Ryman Football League Supporters' Guide and Yearbook 2012

EDITOR
John Robinson

Second Edition

For details of our range of over 1,900 books and 400 DVDs, visit our web site or contact us using the information shown below.

British Library Cataloguing in Publication Data
A catalogue record for this book is available from the British Library

ISBN: 978-1-86223-224-2

Copyright © 2011, SOCCER BOOKS LIMITED (01472 696226)
72 St. Peter's Avenue, Cleethorpes, N.E. Lincolnshire, DN35 8HU, England
Web site   http://www.soccer-books.co.uk
e-mail   info@soccer-books.co.uk

All rights are reserved. No part of this publication may be reproduced, stored in a retrieval system or transmitted, in any form or by any means, electronic, mechanical, photocopying, recording, or otherwise, without the prior written permission of Soccer Books Limited.

The Publishers, and the Football Clubs itemised are unable to accept liability for any loss, damage or injury caused by error or inaccuracy in the information published in this guide.

Printed and bound in the UK by 4edge Ltd, Hockley.

FOREWORD

The "Supporters' Guide" series of books began life as "The Travelling Supporters' Guide" in 1982 and a separate guide covering the top two tiers of the Non-League pyramid has been published by Soccer Books Limited for almost 20 years! However, this is only the second edition of a Supporters' Guide dealing solely with clubs in the Isthmian Football League (sponsored by Ryman), and we hope that it is well received.

We have been unable to visit every ground in the course of preparing this guide and, as a consequence, some of the ground photographs are not as up to date as we would have liked. However, if any reader wishes to submit suitable ground photographs for inclusion in future editions, please contact us at the address shown on the facing page.

Where we use the term 'Child' for concessionary prices, this is often also the price charged to Senior Citizens.

The fixtures listed later in this book were released just a short time before we went to print and, as such, some of the dates shown may be subject to change. We therefore suggest that readers treat these fixtures as a rough guide and check dates carefully before attending matches.

Finally, we would like to wish our readers a safe and happy spectating season.

John Robinson
EDITOR

ACKNOWLEDGEMENTS

In the short time since we embarked upon the preparation of this guide, we have been greatly impressed by the cooperation extended to us by many individuals within the clubs themselves.

Consequently, our thanks go to the numerous club officials who have aided us in the compilation of information contained in this guide and particularly to Kellie Discipline of the Ryman Football League for her assistance.

Our thanks also go to Michael Robinson (page layouts), Bob Budd (cover artwork), Tony Brown (Cup Statistics – www.soccerdata.com). We would also like to thank Dave Twydell, Derek Mead, Chris Bush (footballgroundz.co.uk), David Bauckham (davidbauckham.photoshelter.com) and Martin Wray (www.footballgroundsinfocus.com) for providing a number of the ground photographs used within this guide.

CONTENTS

The Ryman Football League Premier Division Club Information 6-28
The Ryman Football League Division One North Club Information 29-51
The Ryman Football League Division One South Club Information 52-74
Results for the Ryman Football League Premier Division 2010/2011 75
Results for the Ryman Football League Division One North 2010/2011 76
Results for the Ryman Football League Division One South 2010/2011 77
Ryman Football League Premier Division
Final Table and Play-off Results 2010/2011 78
Ryman Football League Division One North and Division One South
Final Tables and Play-off Results 2010/2011 79
2010/2011 F.A. Trophy Results 80-85
2010/2011 F.A. Vase Results 86-90
England Internationals 2010-2011 91-92
Fixtures for the Ryman Football League Premier Division 2011/2012 93
Fixtures for the Ryman Football League Division One North 2011/2012 94
Fixtures for the Ryman Football League Division One South 2011/2012 95
Advertisement: The First 100 Years of the Isthmian Football League 96
Advertisement: The Non-League Football Tables Series 97
Advertisement: The Supporters' Guide Series 98

THE RYMAN FOOTBALL LEAGUE PREMIER DIVISION

Secretary Kellie Discipline   **Phone** (01322) 314999

Address The Base, Dartford Business Park, Victoria Road, Dartford DA1 5FS

Web Site   www.isthmian.co.uk

Clubs for the 2011/2012 Season

AFC Hornchurch	Page 7
Aveley FC	Page 8
Billericay Town FC	Page 9
Bury Town FC	Page 10
Canvey Island FC	Page 11
Carshalton Athletic FC	Page 12
Concord Rangers FC	Page 13
Cray Wanderers FC	Page 14
East Thurrock United FC	Page 15
Harrow Borough FC	Page 16
Hastings United FC	Page 17
Hendon FC	Page 18
Horsham FC	Page 19
Kingstonian FC	Page 20
Leatherhead FC	Page 21
Lewes FC	Page 22
Lowestoft Town FC	Page 23
Margate FC	Page 24
Metropolitan Police FC	Page 25
Tooting & Mitcham United FC	Page 26
Wealdstone FC	Page 27
Wingate & Finchley FC	Page 28

AFC HORNCHURCH

Founded: 1923
Former Names: Hornchurch & Upminster FC and Hornchurch FC
Nickname: 'Urchins'
Ground: The Stadium, Bridge Avenue, Upminster, RM14 2LX
Record Attendance: 3,000 (vs Chelmsford 1966/67)

Colours: Red and White striped shirts, White shorts
Telephone Nº: (01708) 220080
Ground Capacity: 3,000
Seating Capacity: 499
Web site: www.urchins.org.uk

GENERAL INFORMATION
Car Parking: 100 spaces available at the ground
Coach Parking: At the ground
Nearest Railway Station: Upminster (10 minutes walk)
Nearest Tube Station: Upminster Bridge (5 minutes walk)
Club Shop: At the ground
Opening Times: Matchdays only
Telephone Nº: (01708) 220080

GROUND INFORMATION
Away Supporters' Entrances & Sections:
No usual segregation

ADMISSION INFO (2011/2012 PRICES)
Adult Standing: £9.00
Adult Seating: £9.00
Senior Citizen Standing: £6.00
Senior Citizen Seating: £6.00
Under-16s Standing: £2.00
Under-16s Seating: £2.00
Programme: £2.00

DISABLED INFORMATION
Wheelchairs: Accommodated
Helpers: Admitted
Prices: £6.00 for the disabled
Disabled Toilets: Available
Contact: (01708) 220080   (Bookings are not necessary)

Travelling Supporters' Information:
Routes: Exit the M25 at Junction 29 and take the A127 towards London. After about 500 yards, take the sliproad signposted for Upminster/Cranham and continue on for about 1 mile. Turn right at the traffic lights by the church and Bridge Avenue is the 2nd turning on the left after about 400 yards.

AVELEY FC

Founded: 1927
Former Names: None
Nickname: 'The Millers'
Ground: Mill Field, Mill Road, Aveley   RM15 4SJ
Record Attendance: 3,741 (27th February 1971)

Colours: Royal Blue shirts and shorts
Telephone Nº: (01708) 865940
Ground Capacity: 4,000
Seating Capacity: 400
Web Site: www.pitchero.com/clubs/aveley

GENERAL INFORMATION
Car Parking: At the ground
Coach Parking: At the ground
Nearest Railway Station: Rainham (2 miles)
Club Shop: At the ground
Opening Times: Matchdays only 2.00pm to 6.00pm
Telephone Nº: (01708) 865940

GROUND INFORMATION
Away Supporters' Entrances & Sections:
No usual segregation

ADMISSION INFO (2011/2012 PRICES)
Adult Standing: £10.00
Adult Seating: £10.00
Senior Citizen Standing: £6.00
Senior Citizen Seating: £6.00
Under-16s Standing: £1.00
Under-16s Seating: £1.00
Programme Price: £2.00

DISABLED INFORMATION
Wheelchairs: Accommodated (but no special facilities)
Helpers: Admitted
Prices: Normal prices apply for the disabled and helpers
Disabled Toilets: None at present
Contact: (01708) 865740   (Bookings are not necessary)

Travelling Supporters' Information:
Routes: Exit the M25 at junction 30 and take the Thames Gateway (A13) towards Aveley. Pass under Purfleet Road flyover then take the next slip road onto the A1306. At the first roundabout, take the 3rd exit, pass over the A13 and at the next roundabout continue straight across into New Road. Take the first turn on the right into Sandy Lane (B1335) then turn right at the next roundabout into Mill Road. The ground is on the left hand side of the road.

BILLERICAY TOWN FC

Founded: 1880
Former Names: None
Nickname: 'Town' 'Blues'
Ground: New Lodge, Blunts Wall Road, Billericay, Essex CM12 9SA
Record Attendance: 3,841 (28th September 1977)

Colours: Shirts are Royal Blue with White trim, shorts are White with Royal Blue trim
Telephone Nº: (01277) 652188
Fax Number: (01277) 652188
Ground Capacity: 3,500
Seating Capacity: 424
Web site: www.billericaytownfc.co.uk

GENERAL INFORMATION
Car Parking: 50 spaces available at the training ground behind the stadium
Coach Parking: Please contact the club for information
Nearest Railway Station: Billericay (½ mile)
Club Shop: At the ground
Opening Times: Matchdays only

GROUND INFORMATION
Away Supporters' Entrances & Sections: No usual segregation

ADMISSION INFO (2011/2012 PRICES)
Adult Standing: £9.50
Adult Seating: £10.50
Senior Citizen Standing: £6.50
Senior Citizen Seating: £7.50
Under-16s Standing: £2.50
Under-16s Seating: £3.50
Programme Price: £1.50

DISABLED INFORMATION
Wheelchairs: Accommodated
Helpers: Admitted
Prices: Same prices as standing admission
Disabled Toilets: Available in the Clubhouse
Contact: (01277) 652188   (Bookings are necessary)

Travelling Supporters' Information:
Route: Exit the M25 at Junction 28 and follow the A129 to Billericay. Turn right at the 1st set of traffic lights into Tye Common Road then 2nd right into Blunts Wall Road and the ground is on the right.
Alternative route: Exit the M25 at Junction 29 and take the A129 road from Basildon into Billericay and turn left at the 2nd set of traffic lights into Tye Common Road. Then as above.

BURY TOWN FC

Founded: 1872
Former Names: None
Nickname: 'The Blues'
Ground: Ram Meadow, Cotton Lane, Bury St. Edmunds IP33 1XP
Record Attendance: 2,500 (1986)

Colours: Blue shirts, shorts and socks
Telephone N°: (01284) 754721
Ground Capacity: 3,500
Seating Capacity: 300
Web Site: www.burytownfc.co.uk

GENERAL INFORMATION
Car Parking: At the ground
Coach Parking: At the ground
Nearest Railway Station: Bury St. Edmunds (½ mile)
Club Shop: At the ground
Opening Times: Matchdays only 2.00pm to 6.00pm
Telephone N°: (01284) 754721

GROUND INFORMATION
Away Supporters' Entrances & Sections:
No usual segregation

ADMISSION INFO (2011/2012 PRICES)
Adult Standing: £10.00
Adult Seating: £10.00
Senior Citizen Standing: £5.00
Senior Citizen Seating: £5.00
Under-16s Standing: £3.00
Under-16s Seating: £3.00
Under-10s Standing/Seating: Free of charge
Programme Price: £2.00

DISABLED INFORMATION
Wheelchairs: Accommodated
Helpers: Admitted
Prices: Normal prices apply for the disabled and helpers
Disabled Toilets: Available
Contact: (01284) 754721 (Bookings are necessary)

Travelling Supporters' Information:
Routes: Take the A14 to Bury St. Edmunds and exit at Junction 43 for Central Bury St. Edmunds, following 'Town Centre' signs. After about 300 yards, take the first exit at the roundabout into Northgate Street and continue to the second set of traffic lights which is a T-junction. Turn left into Mustow Street then left again into Cotton Lane. The ground is at the bottom of the lane through the council car park.

CANVEY ISLAND FC

Founded: 1926
Former Names: None
Nickname: 'Gulls'
Ground: Park Lane, Canvey Island, Essex SS8 7PX
Record Attendance: 3,553 (15th April 2003)
Pitch Size: 110 × 80 yards

Colours: Yellow shirts with Sky Blue shorts
Telephone Nº: (01268) 682991
Ground Capacity: 4,000
Seating Capacity: 500
Web site: www.canveyislandfc.com

GENERAL INFORMATION
Car Parking: 80 spaces available at the ground
Coach Parking: At the ground as required
Nearest Railway Station: South Benfleet (2 miles)
Club Shop: At the ground
Opening Times: Matchdays plus Thursday and Friday evenings
Telephone Nº: (01268) 682991

GROUND INFORMATION
Away Supporters' Entrances & Sections:
Segregation only used when there is a large away support

ADMISSION INFO (2011/2012 PRICES)
Adult Standing: £10.00
Adult Seating: £10.00
Under-16s/Student/Senior Citizen Standing: £5.00
Under-16s/Student/Senior Citizen Seating: £5.00
Note: Under-12s are admitted for £1.00 when accompanied by a paying adult
Programme Price: £2.00

DISABLED INFORMATION
Wheelchairs: Accommodated
Helpers: Admitted
Prices: Concessionary prices apply for the disabled
Disabled Toilets: None
Contact: (01268) 682991 (Bookings are necessary)

Travelling Supporters' Information:
Routes: Take the M25 to either the A127 or the A13 (recommended) then follow the A13 towards Basildon and Southend. At the multiple roundabout system, follow signs for Canvey Island on the A130 towards the Town Centre. Keep to the left hand lane through the one-way system for approximately 1½ miles. Continue past the old bus garage and Park Lane is the first turning on the right.

CARSHALTON ATHLETIC FC

Founded: 1905
Former Names: None
Nickname: 'The Robins'
Ground: War Memorial Sports Ground, Colston Avenue, Carshalton SM5 2PW
Record Attendance: 7,800 vs Wimbledon
Colours: White shirts with Maroon trim, Maroon shorts
Telephone Nº: (020) 8642-8658
Ground Capacity: 5,000
Seating Capacity: 240
Web site: www.carshaltonathletic.co.uk

GENERAL INFORMATION
Car Parking: 80 spaces available at the ground
Coach Parking: At the ground
Nearest Railway Station: Carshalton (200 yards)
Club Shop: At the ground
Opening Times: Matchdays only
Postal Sales: Yes

GROUND INFORMATION
Away Supporters' Entrances & Sections:
No usual segregation

ADMISSION INFO (2011/2012 PRICES)
Adult Standing/Seating: £10.00
Concessionary Standing/Seating: £6.00
Under-18s Standing/Seating: £3.00
Under-16s Standing/Seating: £1.00
Programme Price: £2.00

DISABLED INFORMATION
Wheelchairs: 6 spaces each for home and away fans are available at the end of the Main Stand
Helpers: Admitted
Prices: Free for the disabled. Helpers usual prices
Disabled Toilets: Available in the Function Hall
Contact: (020) 8642-8658   (Bookings are necessary)

Travelling Supporters' Information:
Routes: From London: Pick up the A23 at The Elephant & Castle or the Oval. Continue along the Brixton Road (A23), through Brixton up Brixton Hill and continue past Streatham Hill to Streatham High Road (still on the A23). At the traffic lights on the junction at St. Leonard's Church, cross into Mitcham Lane (A216), continue through Streatham Road and bear left at the traffic lights at Figgs Marsh onto London Road (A217) and follow A217 through Bishopsford Road until reaching the Rose Hill roundabout. At the roundabout, take the 1st exit into Wrythe Lane and continue for 1 mile, then turn right into Colston Avenue just before the railway bridge. The ground is 50 yards on the right. A private road leads to the Stadium and car park; From the M25: Exit at Junction 8 onto the A217 passing Lower Kingswood, Kingswood Burgh Heath and Banstead until the roundabout before the sign to Sutton. Bear left, still on the A217 to the Rose Hill roundabout, take the 4th exit, then as above.

CONCORD RANGERS FC

Founded: 1967
Former Names: None
Nickname: 'Beach Boys'
Ground: Thames Road, Canvey Island   SS8 0HH
Record Attendance: 1,500

Colours: Yellow shirts with Blue shorts
Telephone Nº: (01268) 515750
Ground Capacity: 1,500
Seating Capacity: 340
Web Site: www.concordrangers.co.uk

GENERAL INFORMATION
Car Parking: At the ground
Coach Parking: At the ground
Nearest Railway Station: Benfleet
Club Shop: Available via the club's web site shortly
Opening Times: –
Telephone Nº: –

GROUND INFORMATION
Away Supporters' Entrances & Sections:
No usual segregation

ADMISSION INFO (2011/2012 PRICES)
Adult Standing: £10.00
Adult Seating: £10.00
Senior Citizen Standing: 5.00
Senior Citizen Seating: £5.00
Under-16s Standing/Seating: Free of charge
Programme Price: £1.00

DISABLED INFORMATION
Wheelchairs: Accommodated
Helpers: Admitted
Prices: Normal prices apply for the disabled and helpers
Disabled Toilets: Available
Contact: (01268) 515750   (Bookings are necessary)

Travelling Supporters' Information:
Routes: Take the A13 to the A130 (Canvey Way) for Canvey Island. At the Benfleet roundabout, take the 3rd exit into Canvey Road and continue along through Charfleets Service Road into Long Road. Take the 5th turn on the right into Thorney Bay Road and Thames Road is the 3rd turn on the right. The ground is on the left-hand side by the oil storage tanks.

CRAY WANDERERS FC

Cray Wanderers are currently groundsharing with Bromley FC

Founded: 1860
Former Names: None
Nickname: 'The Wands'
Ground: The Courage Stadium, Hayes Lane, Bromley BR2 9EF
Record Attendance: 1,523 (1979/80 season)

Colours: Black and Amber shirts with Black shorts
Telephone N°: (020) 8460-5291
Ground Capacity: 3,700
Seating Capacity: 1,300
Web Site: www.craywands.co.uk

GENERAL INFORMATION
Car Parking: 300 spaces available at the ground
Coach Parking: At the ground
Nearest Railway Station: Bromley South (1 mile)
Nearest Bus Station: High Street, Bromley
Club Shop: At the ground
Opening Times: Matchdays only – 1 hour before kick-off and during half-time
Telephone N°: –

GROUND INFORMATION
Away Supporters' Entrances & Sections:
No usual segregation

ADMISSION INFO (2011/2012 PRICES)
Adult Standing: £10.00
Adult Seating: £10.00
Senior Citizen/Junior Standing: £4.00
Senior Citizen/Junior Seating: £4.00
Programme Price: £2.00

DISABLED INFORMATION
Wheelchairs: Accommodated
Helpers: Admitted
Prices: Normal prices apply for the disabled and helpers
Disabled Toilets: Available
Contact: (020) 8460-5291 (Bookings are necessary)

Travelling Supporters' Information:
Routes: Exit the M25 at Junction 4 and follow the A21 for Bromley and London for approximately 4 miles before forking left onto the A232 signposted for Croydon/Sutton. At the second set of traffic lights turn right into Baston Road (B265) and follow for approximately 2 miles as it becomes Hayes Street and then Hayes Lane. The ground is on the right just after a mini-roundabout.

EAST THURROCK UNITED FC

Founded: 1969
Former Names: None
Nickname: 'The Rocks'
Ground: Rookery Hill, Corringham, Essex, SS17 9LB
Record Attendance: 1,250 (vs Woking, 2003)
Pitch Size: 110 × 72 yards
Colours: Amber shirts with Black shorts
Telephone No: (01375) 644166
Ground Capacity: 3,500
Seating Capacity: 250
Web: www.pitchero.com/clubs/eastthurrockunited

GENERAL INFORMATION
Car Parking: At the ground
Coach Parking: At the ground
Nearest Railway Station: Stanford-le-Hope (2 miles)
Nearest Bus Station: Stanford-le-Hope (2 miles)
Club Shop: None
Opening Times: –

GROUND INFORMATION
Away Supporters' Entrances & Sections:
No usual segregation

ADMISSION INFO (2011/2012 PRICES)
Adult Standing: £9.00
Adult Seating: £9.00
Senior Citizen Standing: £4.00
Senior Citizen Seating: £4.00
Under-16s Standing: £1.00
Under-16s Seating: £1.00
Programme Price: £1.00

DISABLED INFORMATION
Wheelchairs: Accommodated
Helpers: Admitted
Prices: Standard prices apply
Disabled Toilets: Available
Contact: 07885 313435 (Bookings are necessary)

Travelling Supporters' Information:
Routes: Exit the M25 at Junction 30 and follow the A13 East. At Stanford-le-Hope turn-off on to the A1014 Coryton, cross over the roundabout and pass through the traffic lights. Then take the first turning on the left signposted Corringham and the ground is immediately on the left.

HARROW BOROUGH FC

Founded: 1933
Former Names: Roxonians FC and Harrow Town FC
Nickname: 'The Boro'
Ground: Earlsmead, Carlyon Avenue, South Harrow, Middlesex HA2 8SS
Record Attendance: 3,000 (1946)

Colours: Shirts are Red with White trim, Red shorts
Telephone Nº: 0844 561-1347
Ground Capacity: 3,068
Seating Capacity: 300
Web site: www.harrowboro.com

GENERAL INFORMATION
Car Parking: 120 spaces available at the ground
Coach Parking: At the ground
Nearest Railway Station: Northolt Park (½ mile)
Nearest Tube Station: South Harrow LRT
Club Shop: Yes – Arundel Drive side of the ground
Opening Times: Open daily during normal licensing hours
Telephone Nº: 0844 561-1347

GROUND INFORMATION
Away Supporters' Entrances & Sections:
Earlsmead side entrances and accommodation

ADMISSION INFO (2011/2012 PRICES)
Adult Standing: £10.00
Adult Seating: £10.00
Senior Citizen Standing: £5.00
Senior Citizen Seating: £5.00
Under-16s Standing: £2.00
Under-16s Seating: £2.00
Programme Price: £2.00

DISABLED INFORMATION
Wheelchairs: 8 spaces are available in the Main Stand
Helpers: Admitted
Prices: Free for the disabled if booked in advance
Disabled Toilets: Available
Contact: 0844 561-1347   (Bookings are necessary)

Travelling Supporters' Information:
Routes: Exit the M25 onto the M40 East and carry on to the A40. Turn left at MacDonalds Northolt and travel past Northolt LRT Station to the traffic lights. Turn left to the roundabout near the Eastcote Arms and then right into Eastcote Lane and right into Carlyon Avenue then finally right again into Earlsmead.

HASTINGS UNITED FC

Founded: 1894
Former Names: Hastings Town FC, Hastings FC and St. Leonard's Amateurs FC
Nickname: 'The U's'
Ground: The Pilot Field, Elphinstone Road, Hastings, TN34 2AX

Record Attendance: 4,888 (1996/97 season)
Colours: Claret and Blue shirts with White shorts
Telephone No: (01424) 444635
Ground Capacity: 4,000
Seating Capacity: 600
Web site: www.hastingsunitedfc.co.uk

GENERAL INFORMATION
Car Parking: Street parking only
Coach Parking: Street parking only
Nearest Railway Station: Hastings (1½ miles)
Club Shop: At the ground
Opening Times: Matchdays only
Telephone No: (01424) 444635

GROUND INFORMATION
Away Supporters' Entrances & Sections:
No usual segregation

ADMISSION INFO (2011/2012 PRICES)
Adult Standing: £9.00
Adult Seating: £9.00
Child Standing: £3.00
Child Seating: £3.00
Senior Citizen Standing: £6.00
Senior Citizen Seating: £6.00
Programme Price: £2.00

DISABLED INFORMATION
Wheelchairs: 6 spaces available in total
Helpers: Please phone the club for information
Prices: Please phone the club for information
Disabled Toilets: Available in the Social Club
Contact: (01424) 444635 (Bookings are not necessary)

Travelling Supporters' Information:
Routes: From the A21 turn left into St. Helens Road (A2101). After 1 mile turn left into St. Helens Park Road which leads into Downs Road. Follow Downs Road to the end then turn left at the T-junction. The ground is on the right.

HENDON FC

Founded: 1908
Former Names: Christchurch Hampstead FC (1908-1909); Hampstead Town FC (1909-26); Hampstead FC (1926-1933); Golders Green FC (1933-1946)
Nickname: 'Dons' 'Greens'
Wembley FC's Ground: Vale Farm, Watford Road, Wembley HA0 3HG
Record Attendance: 9,000 (at the old ground – 1952)

Colours: Green shirts with White shorts
Telephone No: (020) 8908-3553
Ground Capacity: 2,450
Seating Capacity: 350
Web site: www.hendonfc.net

GENERAL INFORMATION
Car Parking: A number of car parks are near to the ground
Coach Parking: At the adjacent car park
Nearest Railway Station: Sudbury & Harrow Road (5 minutes walk)
Nearest Tube Station: Sudbury Town (¾ mile)
Club Shop: At the ground
Opening Times: Matchdays only
Telephone No: (020) 8908-3553

GROUND INFORMATION
Away Supporters' Entrances & Sections: No usual segregation

ADMISSION INFO (2011/2012 PRICES)
Adult Standing and Seating: £9.00
Concessionary Standing and Seating: £5.00
Under-16s Standing and Seating: £1.00
Programme Price: £1.50

DISABLED INFORMATION
Wheelchairs: Accommodated
Helpers: One helper admitted per wheelchair
Prices: Free for each helper with a disabled fan. Extra helpers are charged half normal prices
Disabled Toilets: Please contact the club for details
Contact: (020) 8908-3553 (Bookings are necessary)

Travelling Supporters' Information:
Routes: Wembley FC's ground is located in Sudbury, within the Vale Farm Sports Ground complex by the side of the A404 Watford Road and close to the junction with the A4005 Harrow Road.

HORSHAM FC

Horsham FC are currently groundsharing with Horsham YMCA FC

Founded: 1881
Former Names: None
Nickname: 'Hornets'
Ground: Goring's Mead, Brighton Road, Horsham, RH13 5BP
Record Attendance: 7,200 vs Notts County (1947)

Colours: Green and Yellow shirts with Green shorts
Telephone Nº: (01403) 266888
Ground Capacity: 1,575
Seating Capacity: 150
Web site: www.hornetsreview.co.uk

GENERAL INFORMATION

Car Parking: None at the ground but various car parks are available around Horsham
Coach Parking: By Police direction
Nearest Railway Station: Horsham (15 minutes walk)
Club Shop: None
Opening Times: –
Telephone Nº: –

GROUND INFORMATION

Away Supporters' Entrances & Sections:
No usual segregation

ADMISSION INFO (2011/2012 PRICES)

Adult Standing: £10.00
Adult Seating: £11.00
Under-16s Standing: £1.00
Under-16s Seating: £2.00
Senior Citizen Standing: £5.00
Senior Citizen Seating: £6.00
Programme Price: £1.50

DISABLED INFORMATION

Wheelchairs: Accommodated
Helpers: Admitted
Prices: Normal prices apply for the disabled and helpers
Disabled Toilets: Available
Contact: (01403) 266888 (Bookings are not necessary)

Travelling Supporters' Information:
Routes: Take the A24 to the Horsham bypass then follow the A281 southbound. Continue along for about 2½ miles and Goring's Mead is the 3rd turning on the right after crossing the railway line.

KINGSTONIAN FC

Founded: 1885
Former Names: Kingston & Surbiton YMCA (1885-1887); Saxons (1887-90); Kingston Wanderers (1890-1893); Kingston on Thames (1893-1908); Old Kingstonians until 1919
Nickname: 'The K's'
Ground: Kingsmeadow Stadium, 422A Jack Goodchild Way, Kingston Road, Kingston-upon-Thames, Surrey KT1 3PB

Record Attendance: 4,582 (1995)
Ground Capacity: 4,720
Seating Capacity: 1,265
Colours: Red and White hooped shirts, Black shorts
Telephone Nº: 07545 927459
Web site: www.kingstonian.net

GENERAL INFORMATION
Car Parking: At the ground
Coach Parking: At the ground
Nearest Railway Station: Norbiton (1 mile)
Club Shop: At the ground
Opening Times: Matchdays only from 1 hour before kick-off until 30 minutes after the final whistle
Telephone Nº: –

GROUND INFORMATION
Away Supporters' Entrances & Sections:
No usual segregation

ADMISSION INFO (2011/2012 PRICES)
Adult Standing/Seating: £10.00
Senior Citizen Standing/Seating: £7.00
Student/Under-21s Standing/Seating: £4.00
Under-16s Standing/Seating: £2.00
Programme Price: £2.00

DISABLED INFORMATION
Wheelchairs: Accommodated around the ground
Helpers: Please phone the club for information
Prices: Please phone the club for information
Disabled Toilets: Yes
Contact: 07545 927459 (Bookings are necessary)

Travelling Supporters' Information:
Routes: Exit the M25 at Junction 10 and take the A3 to the New Malden/Worcester Park turn-off and turn into Malden Road (A2043). Follow Malden Road to the mini-roundabout and turn left into Kingston Road. Kingsmeadow is situated approximately 1 mile up the Kingston Road, on the left-hand side and is signposted from the mini-roundabout.

LEATHERHEAD FC

Founded: 1907
Former Names: Leatherhead Rose FC and Leatherhead United FC
Nickname: 'The Tanners'
Ground: Fetcham Grove, Guildford Road, Leatherhead KT22 9AS

Record Attendance: 5,500 (1976)
Colours: Green shirts with White shorts
Telephone No: (01372) 360151
Ground Capacity: 3,400
Seating Capacity: 200
Web Site: www.leatherheadfc-online.co.uk

GENERAL INFORMATION
Car Parking: At the ground
Coach Parking: At the ground
Nearest Railway Station: Leatherhead (¼ mile)
Club Shop: At the ground
Opening Times: Matchdays only from 1 hour before kick-off
Telephone No: –

GROUND INFORMATION
Away Supporters' Entrances & Sections:
No usual segregation

ADMISSION INFO (2011/2012 PRICES)
Adult Standing: £10.00
Adult Seating: £10.00
Senior Citizen Standing: £5.00
Senior Citizen Seating: £5.00
Under-16s Standing/Seating: £3.00
Programme Price: £2.00

DISABLED INFORMATION
Wheelchairs: Accommodated
Helpers: Admitted
Prices: Normal prices apply for the disabled and helpers
Disabled Toilets: Available
Contact: (01372) 360151   (Bookings are necessary)

Travelling Supporters' Information:
Routes: Exit the M25 at Junction 9 and take the Bypass Road into Leatherhead. At the next roundabout, turn left into Kingston Road, continue along into Bull Hill then bear right along Station Road. Turn left into Waterway Road, continue straight on at the mini-roundabout then take the next turning on the left for Fetcham Grove.

LEWES FC

Founded: 1885
Former Names: None
Nickname: 'Rooks'
Ground: The Dripping Pan, Mountfield Road, Lewes BN7 2XD
Record Attendance: 2,500 (vs Newhaven 26/12/47)
Pitch Size: 109 × 74 yards

Colours: Red & Black striped shirts with Black shorts
Telephone No: (01273) 472100
Fax Number: (01273) 483210
Ground Capacity: 3,000
Seating Capacity: 500
Web site: www.lewesfc.com

GENERAL INFORMATION
Supporters Club: c/o Club
Telephone No: (01273) 472100
Car Parking: At the ground
Coach Parking: At Lewes Railway Station (adjacent)
Nearest Railway Station: Lewes (adjacent)
Nearest Bus Station: Lewes (½ mile)
Club Shop: At the ground.
Opening Times: Matchdays only

GROUND INFORMATION
Away Supporters' Entrances & Sections:
No usual segregation – otherwise as directed by stewards

ADMISSION INFO (2011/2012 PRICES)
Adult Standing: £10.00
Adult Seating: £10.00
Junior (Under-14s) Standing: £2.00
Junior (Under-14s) Seating: £2.00
Senior Citizen/Under-16s Standing: £5.00
Senior Citizen/Under-16s Seating: £5.00
Programme Price: £2.00

DISABLED INFORMATION
Wheelchairs: Accommodated
Helpers: Admitted
Prices: Normal prices apply for the disabled and helpers
Disabled Toilets: Available
Contact: (01273) 472100

Travelling Supporters' Information:
Routes: From the North: Take the A26 or the A275 to Lewes and follow signs for the Railway Station. Pass the station on the left and take the next left. The ground is adjacent; From the South and West: Take the A27 to the A26 for the Town Centre. Then as above.

LOWESTOFT TOWN FC

Founded: 1880
Former Names: East Suffolk FC
Nickname: 'The Trawler Boys'
Ground: Crown Meadow, Love Road, Lowestoft, NR32 2PA
Record Attendance: 5,000 (1967)

Colours: Blue shirts and shorts
Telephone Nº: (01502) 573818
Ground Capacity: 2,250
Seating Capacity: 466
Web Site: www.lowestofttownfc.co.uk

GENERAL INFORMATION
Car Parking: Street parking only
Coach Parking: By Police direction
Nearest Railway Station: Lowestoft (½ mile)
Club Shop: At the ground
Opening Times: Matchdays only 11.00am to 11.00pm
Telephone Nº: (01502) 567280

GROUND INFORMATION
Away Supporters' Entrances & Sections:
No usual segregation

ADMISSION INFO (2011/2012 PRICES)
Adult Standing: £10.00
Adult Seating: £10.00
Senior Citizen Standing: £8.00
Senior Citizen Seating: £8.00
Under-16s Standing: £4.00
Under-16s Seating: £4.00
Programme Price: £2.00

DISABLED INFORMATION
Wheelchairs: Accommodated
Helpers: Admitted
Prices: Normal prices apply for the disabled and helpers
Disabled Toilets: Available
Contact: 07930 872947 (Bookings are necessary)

Travelling Supporters' Information:
Routes: Take the A146 or the A12 to Lowestoft Town Centre then head north on the A12 Katwijk Way Road. Turn left into Love Road for the ground.

MARGATE FC

Founded: 1896
Former Names: Thanet United FC
Nickname: 'The Gate'
Ground: Hartsdown Park, Hartsdown Road, Margate CT9 5QZ
Record Attendance: 14,500 vs Spurs (1973)

Colours: Royal Blue shirts and shorts
Telephone N°: (01843) 221769
Fax Number: (01843) 221769
Ground Capacity: 2,000
Seating Capacity: 350
Web site: www.margate-fc.com

GENERAL INFORMATION
Car Parking: Street parking
Coach Parking: Available at the ground
Nearest Railway Station: Margate (10 minutes walk)
Club Shop: At the ground
Opening Times: Matchdays only
Telephone N°: (01843) 225566

GROUND INFORMATION
Away Supporters' Entrances & Sections:
Segregation only used for selected fixtures

ADMISSION INFO (2011/2012 PRICES)
Adult Standing: £10.00
Adult Seating: £11.00
Under-16s Standing: £3.00
Under-16s Seating: £4.00
Senior Citizen Standing: £7.00
Senior Citizen Seating: £8.00
Programme Price: £2.00

DISABLED INFORMATION
Wheelchairs: Accommodated
Helpers: Admitted
Prices: Concessionary prices apply
Disabled Toilets: Available
Contact: (01843) 221769   (Bookings are necessary)

Travelling Supporters' Information:
Routes: Take the M2/A2 to the A299 then the A28 (Thanet Way) into Margate, turn right opposite the Dog & Duck Pub into Hartsdown Road. Proceed over the crossroads and the ground is on the left.

METROPOLITAN POLICE FC

Founded: 1919
Former Names: None
Nickname: 'The Blues'
Ground: Imber Court, Metropolitan Police Sports Club, Embercourt Road, East Molesey KT8 0BT
Record Attendance: 4,500 (1934)
Colours: Blue shirts and shorts
Telephone Nº: (020) 8398-7358
Fax Number: (01932) 782215
Ground Capacity: 3,000
Seating Capacity: 297
Web Site: www.metpolicefc.co.uk

GENERAL INFORMATION
Car Parking: At the ground
Coach Parking: At the ground
Nearest Railway Station: Thames Ditton (½ mile)
Nearest Tube Station: Richmond (7 miles)
Club Shop: None
Opening Times: –
Telephone Nº: –

GROUND INFORMATION
Away Supporters' Entrances & Sections:
No usual segregation

ADMISSION INFO (2011/2012 PRICES)
Adult Standing: £9.00
Adult Seating: £9.00
Senior Citizen/Junior Standing: £4.00
Senior Citizen/Junior Seating: £4.00
Programme Price: £1.50

DISABLED INFORMATION
Wheelchairs: Accommodated
Helpers: Admitted
Prices: £4.00 in total for each disabled fan and helper
Disabled Toilets: Available in the Clubhouse
Contact: 07961 334523   (Bookings are not necessary)

Travelling Supporters' Information:
Routes: Follow the A3 northwards from Central London or M25 Junction 10, then take the A309 to the Scilly Isles roundabout. Continue along the A309 into Hampton Court Way then turn left at the next roundabout into Ember Court Road. The Ground is straight ahead at the end of Ember Court Road.

TOOTING & MITCHAM UNITED FC

Founded: 1932
Former Names: None
Nickname: 'Terrors'
Ground: Imperial Fields, Bishopsford Road, Morden, SM4 6BF
Record Attendance: 2,367 (1st April 2005)

Colours: Black & White striped shirts with Black shorts
Telephone No: (020) 8685-6193
Fax Number: (020) 8685-6190
Ground Capacity: 3,500
Seating Capacity: 600
Web Site: www.thehubattmufc.co.uk

GENERAL INFORMATION
Car Parking: At the ground
Coach Parking: At the ground
Nearest Railway Station: Mitcham Junction (1½ miles)
Nearest Tube Station: Morden (1½ miles)
Club Shop: At the ground
Opening Times: Matchdays only
Telephone No: –

GROUND INFORMATION
Away Supporters' Entrances & Sections:
No usual segregation

ADMISSION INFO (2011/2012 PRICES)
Adult Standing: £10.00
Adult Seating: £10.00
Senior Citizen/Student Standing: £5.00
Senior Citizen/Student Seating: £5.00
Under-16s Standing/Seating: £1.00
Programme Price: £2.00

DISABLED INFORMATION
Wheelchairs: Accommodated
Helpers: Admitted
Prices: Normal prices apply for the disabled. Free of charge for helpers
Disabled Toilets: Available
Contact: (020) 8685-6193   (Bookings are not necessary)

Travelling Supporters' Information:
Routes: Exit the M25 at Junction 8 and take the A217 towards London. At the major Rose Hill Roundabout (which also has traffic lights), take the 3rd exit for Mitcham which is still the A217 but is named Bishopsford Road. Continue for about a mile, passing through two sets of traffic lights and the ground is situated on the right, opposite a petrol station.

WEALDSTONE FC

Photo courtesy of Steve Foster/Wealdstone FC

Founded: 1899
Former Names: None
Nickname: 'The Stones'
Ground: St. George's Stadium, Grosvenor Vale, Ruislip HA4 6JQ
Record Attendance: 1,638 (vs Rotherham United)
Colours: Shirts and shorts are Blue with White trim

Telephone Nº: 07790 038095
Fax Number: (020) 8930-7143
Correspondence Address: 31 Jersey Avenue, Stanmore HA7 2JG
Ground Capacity: 2,387
Seating Capacity: 315
Web site: www.wealdstone-fc.com

GENERAL INFORMATION
Car Parking: 100 spaces available at the ground
Coach Parking: Available outside the ground
Nearest Mainline Station: West Ruislip (1 mile)
Nearest Tube Station: Ruislip (½ mile)
Club Shop: Yes
Opening Times: Orders through the post only
Telephone Nº: –

GROUND INFORMATION
Away Supporters' Entrances & Sections:
No usual segregation

ADMISSION INFO (2011/2012 PRICES)
Adult Standing: £10.00
Adult Seating: £10.00
Senior Citizen Standing: £5.00
Senior Citizen Seating: £5.00
Under-16s Standing/Seating: £2.00
Programme Price: £2.00

DISABLED INFORMATION
Wheelchairs: Accommodated
Helpers: Admitted
Prices: Normal prices apply
Disabled Toilets: Available
Contact: (01895) 637487

Travelling Supporters' Information:
Routes: Exit the M25 at Junction 16 and take the A40 towards Uxbridge. At the Polish War Memorial Junction with the A4180, follow the Ruislip signs (West End Road). After about 1½ miles, turn right into Grosvenor Vale for the ground.

WINGATE & FINCHLEY FC

Founded: 1874 (as Finchley FC)
Former Names: Formed by the amalgamation of Finchley FC and Wingate FC in 1991
Nickname: 'The Blues'
Ground: The Harry Abrahams Stadium, Summers Lane, Finchley, London N12 0PD
Record Attendance: 9,555 (1949/50 season)

Colours: Azure Blue shirts with White shorts
Telephone Nº: (020) 8446-2217
Fax Number: (020) 8343-8194
Ground Capacity: 8,500
Seating Capacity: 500
Web Site: www.wingatefinchley.com

GENERAL INFORMATION
Car Parking: Street parking only
Coach Parking: At the ground
Nearest Railway Station: New Southgate (2 miles)
Nearest Tube Station: West Finchley (1 mile)
Club Shop: None
Opening Times: –
Telephone Nº: –

GROUND INFORMATION
Away Supporters' Entrances & Sections:
No usual segregation

ADMISSION INFO (2011/2012 PRICES)
Adult Standing: £10.00
Adult Seating: £10.00
Senior Citizen/Student Standing: £5.00
Senior Citizen/Student Seating: £5.00
Note: Under-16s are admitted free of charge
Programme Price: £2.00

DISABLED INFORMATION
Wheelchairs: Accommodated
Helpers: Admitted
Prices: Normal prices apply for the disabled and helpers
Disabled Toilets: None
Contact: (020) 8446-2217 (Bookings are not necessary)

Travelling Supporters' Information:
Routes: Exit the A406 North Circular Road at the junction with the A1000 (High Road) and head northwards. After approximately 300 yards, turn right into Summers Lane and the Stadium is on the right hand side of the road just after the Fitness Centre.

THE RYMAN FOOTBALL LEAGUE DIVISION ONE NORTH

Secretary Kellie Discipline   **Phone** (01322) 314999

Address The Base, Dartford Business Park, Victoria Road, Dartford DA1 5FS

Web Site www.isthmian.co.uk

Clubs for the 2011/2012 Season

AFC Sudbury	Page 30
Brentwood Town FC	Page 31
Chatham Town FC	Page 32
Cheshunt FC	Page 33
Enfield Town FC	Page 34
Grays Athletic FC	Page 35
Great Wakering Rovers FC	Page 36
Harlow Town FC	Page 37
Heybridge Swifts FC	Page 38
Leiston FC	Page 39
Leyton FC	Page 40
Maldon & Tiptree FC	Page 41
Needham Market FC	Page 42
Potters Bar Town FC	Page 43
Redbridge FC	Page 44
Romford FC	Page 45
Soham Town Rangers FC	Page 46
Thamesmead Town FC	Page 47
Tilbury FC	Page 48
Waltham Abbey FC	Page 49
Waltham Forest FC	Page 50
Ware FC	Page 51

AFC SUDBURY

Founded: 1999
Former Names: Formed by the amalgamation of Sudbury Town FC and Sudbury Wanderers FC in 1999
Nickname: 'Yellows'
Ground: The MEL Group Stadium, Brundon Lane, Sudbury CO10 7HJ
Record Attendance: 1,407 (vs Maldon in 2003)

Colours: Yellow shirts with Blue shorts
Telephone Nº: (01787) 376213
Ground Capacity: 2,500
Seating Capacity: 200
Web Site: www.afcsudbury.com

GENERAL INFORMATION
Car Parking: At the ground
Coach Parking: At the ground
Nearest Railway Station: Sudbury (1½ miles)
Club Shop: At the ground
Opening Times: Matchdays only
Telephone Nº: (01787) 376213

GROUND INFORMATION
Away Supporters' Entrances & Sections:
No usual segregation

ADMISSION INFO (2011/2012 PRICES)
Adult Standing: £8.00
Adult Seating: £8.00
Senior Citizen Standing: £5.00
Senior Citizen Seating: £5.00
Note: Under-14s are admitted free of charge when accompanied by a paying adult
Programme Price: £1.50

DISABLED INFORMATION
Wheelchairs: Accommodated
Helpers: Admitted
Prices: Normal prices apply for the disabled and helpers
Disabled Toilets: Available
Contact: (01787) 376213 (Bookings are not necessary)

Travelling Supporters' Information:
Routes: From the South: Take the A131 to Sudbury. On descending the hill into Sudbury, turn left at first set of traffic lights (by the Kings Head), and then take the first right into Brundon Lane. The road narrows before reaching ground on the right hand side; From the North: Enter Sudbury and follow signs for Halstead/Chelmsford. Cross the river bridge and pass under the old rail bridge, then turn right at the traffic lights (Kings Head) into Bulmer Road and the first right again into Brundon Lane.
Sat Nav: Use postcode CO10 7HN

BRENTWOOD TOWN FC

Founded: 1954
Former Names: None
Nickname: 'The Blues'
Ground: The Arena, The Brentwood Centre, Doddinghurst Road, Brentwood CM15 9NN
Record Attendance: 1,050 (September 2008)

Colours: Sky Blue shirts with Navy Blue shorts
Telephone Nº: 0776 800-6370
Fax Number: (01708) 437904
Ground Capacity: 2,000
Seating Capacity: 150
Web Site: www.brentwoodtownfc.co.uk

GENERAL INFORMATION
Car Parking: At the ground
Coach Parking: At the ground
Nearest Railway Station: Brentwood (1¾ miles)
Club Shop: At the ground
Opening Times: Matchdays only
Telephone Nº: –

GROUND INFORMATION
Away Supporters' Entrances & Sections:
No usual segregation

ADMISSION INFO (2011/2012 PRICES)
Adult Standing: £8.50
Adult Seating: £8.50
Senior Citizen Standing/Seating: £4.00
Junior Standing/Seating: £1.00
Programme Price: Included in admission price

DISABLED INFORMATION
Wheelchairs: Accommodated
Helpers: Admitted
Prices: Normal prices apply for the disabled and helpers
Disabled Toilets: Available
Contact: 0776 800-6370   (Bookings are necessary)

Travelling Supporters' Information:
Routes: Exit the M25 at Junction 28 and (avoiding the A12 bypass) take the A1023 (Brook Street) into Brentwood. After about 1½ miles this becomes Brentwood High Street and, at the eastern end, turn left into Ongar Road then fork right at the 3rd mini-roundabout into Doddinghurst Road. The Brentwood Centre is on the right after approximately ½ mile.

CHATHAM TOWN FC

Founded: 1882
Former Names: None
Nickname: 'The Chats'
Ground: Maidstone Road Sports Ground, Bournville Avenue, Chatham ME4 6LR
Record Attendance: 5,000 (1980)

Colours: Red shirts and Black shorts
Telephone Nº: (01634) 812194
Ground Capacity: 2,000
Seating Capacity: 600
Web Site: www.chathamtownfc.net

GENERAL INFORMATION
Car Parking: At the ground
Coach Parking: At the ground
Nearest Railway Station: Chatham (½ mile)
Club Shop: At the ground
Opening Times: Matchdays only
Telephone Nº: (01634) 812194

GROUND INFORMATION
Away Supporters' Entrances & Sections:
No segregation

ADMISSION INFO (2011/2012 PRICES)
Adult Standing/Seating: £8.00
Senior Citizen/Student Standing/Seating: £4.00
Under-16s Standing/Seating: £2.00
Programme Price: £2.00

DISABLED INFORMATION
Wheelchairs: Accommodated
Helpers: Admitted
Prices: Normal prices apply for the disabled and helpers
Disabled Toilets: Available
Contact: (01634) 812194   (Bookings are not necessary)

Travelling Supporters' Information:
Routes: Exit the M2 at Junction 3, and follow directions for Chatham & Town Centre, following the A229. Pass a Homebase & Toys 'R' Us on the left hand side. At the fork in the road, bear right onto the A230 Maidstone Road. Continue along Maidstone Road, go straight on at the cross roads and you will see a petrol station on the left. Bournville Avenue is opposite the petrol station on the right hand side of the road and, in Bournville Avenue, the entrance to the ground is the first turn on the left.

CHESHUNT FC

Founded: 1946
Former Names: Cheshunt Sports FC
Nickname: 'The Ambers'
Ground: Cheshunt Stadium, Theobalds Lane, Cheshunt EN8 8RU
Record Attendance: 5,000 (vs Bromley – 1950)
Pitch Size: 112 × 78 yards

Colours: Amber shirts with Black shorts
Telephone No: (01992) 633500
Ground Capacity: 5,000
Seating Capacity: 285
Web site: www.theambers.co.uk

GENERAL INFORMATION
Car Parking: At the ground
Coach Parking: At the ground
Nearest Railway Station: Theobalds Grove (¼ mile)
Nearest Bus Station: Waltham Cross
Club Shop: None – but some items are available for purchase from the bar at the Social Club

GROUND INFORMATION
Away Supporters' Entrances & Sections:
No usual segregation

ADMISSION INFO (2011/2012 PRICES)
Adult Standing/Seating: £7.00
Concessionary Standing/Seating: £3.50
Under-16s Standing/Seating: £1.00
Programme Price: £1.50

DISABLED INFORMATION
Wheelchairs: Accommodated
Helpers: Admitted
Prices: Normal prices apply
Disabled Toilets: Access to Clubhouse toilets is available
Contact: (01992) 626752 (Bookings are not necessary)

Travelling Supporters' Information:
Routes: Exit the M25 at Junction 25 and take the A1 northwards towards Hertford. Take the 3rd exit at the first roundabout then turn left at the traffic lights and pass under the railway bridge. Take the next turning on the left into Theobalds Lane and the ground is situated on the right after ¼ mile.

ENFIELD TOWN FC

Enfield Town FC are currently groundsharing with Cheshunt FC but hope to move to the Queen Elizabeth Stadium during the 2011/2012 season. Please contact the club for further information.

Founded: 2001
Former Names: None
Nickname: 'Towners'
Ground: Cheshunt Stadium, Theobalds Lane, Cheshunt EN8 8RU
Record Attendance: 562 (at Enfield)
Pitch Size: 112 × 78 yards

Colours: White shirts with Royal Blue shorts
Telephone N°: (020) 8804-5491
Fax Number: (020) 8804-5491
Ground Capacity: 5,000
Seating Capacity: 285
Web Site: www.etfc.co.uk

GENERAL INFORMATION
Car Parking: At the ground
Coach Parking: At the ground
Nearest Railway Station: Theobalds Grove (¼ mile)
Nearest Bus Station: Waltham Cross
Club Shop: At the ground
Opening Times: Matchdays only
Telephone N°: –

GROUND INFORMATION
Away Supporters' Entrances & Sections:
No usual segregation

ADMISSION INFO (2011/2012 PRICES)
Adult Standing/Seating: £8.00
Senior Citizen Standing/Seating: £5.00
Under-16s Standing/Seating: £1.00
Programme Price: £2.00

DISABLED INFORMATION
Wheelchairs: Accommodated
Helpers: Admitted
Prices: Normal prices apply for the disabled and helpers
Disabled Toilets: Available
Contact: (020) 8804-5491 (Bookings are not necessary)

Travelling Supporters' Information:
Routes: Exit the M25 at Junction 25 and take the A1 northwards towards Hertford. Take the 3rd exit at the first roundabout then turn left at the traffic lights and pass under the railway bridge. Take the next turning on the left into Theobalds Lane and the ground is situated on the right after ¼ mile.

GRAYS ATHLETIC FC

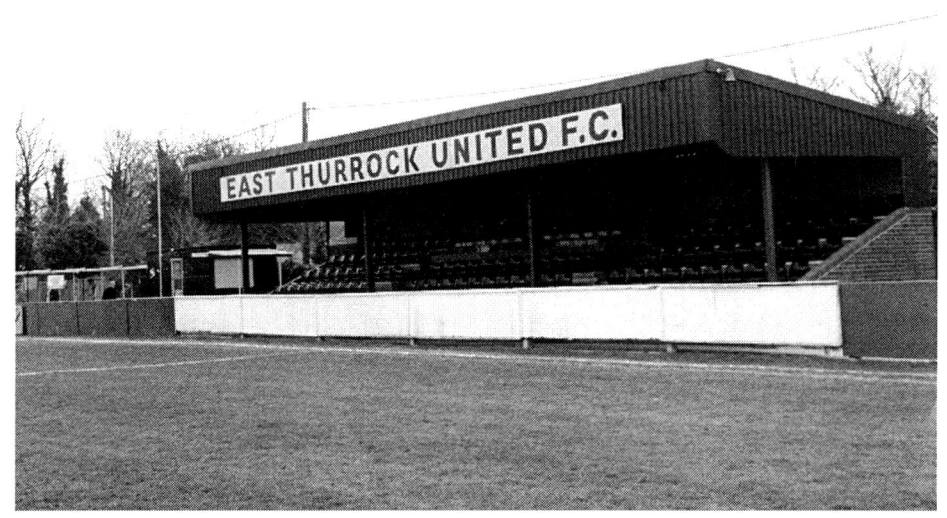

Grays Athletic FC are groundsharing with East Thurrock United FC during the 2011/2012 season.

Founded: 1890
Former Names: None
Nickname: 'The Blues'
Ground: Rookery Hill, Corringham, Essex, SS17 9LB
Record Attendance: 9,500 (at Grays during 1959)
Pitch Size: 110 × 72 yards
Colours: Royal Blue shirts and shorts
Daytime Telephone Nº: (020) 8502-8950
Evenings Contact Nº: 07931 731358
Ground Capacity: 3,500
Seating Capacity: 250
Web site: www.graysathletic.co.uk

GENERAL INFORMATION
Car Parking: At the ground
Coach Parking: At the ground
Nearest Railway Station: Stanford-le-Hope (2 miles)
Nearest Bus Station: Stanford-le-Hope (2 miles)
Club Shop: At the ground
Opening Times: Matchdays only

GROUND INFORMATION
Away Supporters' Entrances & Sections:
No usual segregation

ADMISSION INFO (2011/2012 PRICES)
Adult Standing: £8.00
Adult Seating: £8.00
Concessionary Standing: £5.00
Concessionary Seating: £5.00
Under-14s Standing: £1.00
Under-14s Seating: £1.00
Programme Price: £2.00

DISABLED INFORMATION
Wheelchairs: Accommodated
Helpers: Admitted
Prices: Please phone the club for further information
Disabled Toilets: Available
Contact: 07931 731358   (Bookings are recommended)

Travelling Supporters' Information:
Routes: Exit the M25 at Junction 30 and follow the A13 East. At Stanford-le-Hope turn-off on to the A1014 Coryton, cross over the roundabout and pass through the traffic lights. Then take the first turning on the left signposted Corringham and the ground is immediately on the left.

GREAT WAKERING ROVERS FC

Founded: 1919
Former Names: None
Nickname: 'The Rovers'
Ground: Burroughs Park, Little Wakering Hall Lane, Great Wakering   SS3 0HH
Record Attendance: 1,150 (19th July 2006)

Colours: Green & White shirts with Green shorts
Telephone Nº: (01702) 217812
Ground Capacity: 2,500
Seating Capacity: 150
Web Site: www.gwrovers.co.uk

GENERAL INFORMATION
Car Parking: At the ground
Coach Parking: At the ground
Nearest Railway Station: Shoeburyness (3 miles)
Club Shop: None
Opening Times: –

GROUND INFORMATION
Away Supporters' Entrances & Sections:
No usual segregation

ADMISSION INFO (2011/2012 PRICES)
Adult Standing: £7.50
Adult Seating: £7.50
Senior Citizen/Junior Standing: £3.50
Senior Citizen/Junior Seating: £3.50
Under-11s Standing: £1.00
Under-11s Seating: £1.00
Programme Price: £1.50

DISABLED INFORMATION
Wheelchairs: Accommodated
Helpers: Admitted
Prices: Normal prices apply for the disabled and helpers
Disabled Toilets: Available
Contact: (01702) 217812   (Bookings are not necessary)

Travelling Supporters' Information:
Routes: Take the A127 to Southend then follow signs for Shoeburyness for about 4 miles. Take the B1017 to Great Wakering and continue along the High Street for about ½ mile before turning left into Little Wakering Hall Lane. The ground is located at the end of the road on the left hand side.

HARLOW TOWN FC

Founded: 1879
Former Names: None
Nickname: 'Hawks'
Ground: Barrows Farm Stadium, Elizabeth Way, Harrow CM19 5BE
Record Attendance: 2,149 (8th November 2008)

Colours: Red shirts and shorts
Telephone Nº: (01279) 445319
Fax Number: (01279) 635846
Ground Capacity: 3,500
Seating Capacity: 400
Web Site: www.pitchero.com/clubs/harlowtownfc

GENERAL INFORMATION
Car Parking: At the ground
Coach Parking: At the ground
Nearest Railway Station: Harlow Town (1¼ miles)
Club Shop: None at present
Opening Times: –
Telephone Nº: –

GROUND INFORMATION
Away Supporters' Entrances & Sections:
No usual segregation

ADMISSION INFO (2011/2012 PRICES)
Adult Standing: £9.00
Adult Seating: £9.00
Senior Citizen Standing: £5.00
Senior Citizen Seating: £5.00
Note: Under-16s are admitted free of charge
Programme Price: £2.00

DISABLED INFORMATION
Wheelchairs: Accommodated
Helpers: Admitted
Prices: Normal prices apply for the disabled and helpers
Disabled Toilets: Available
Contact: (01279) 445319 (Bookings are not necessary)

Travelling Supporters' Information:
Routes: Exit the M11 at Junction 7, take the A414 to Harlow then turn left at the roundabout onto the A1169 Southern Way. Continue along the A1169 signed for Roydon into Katherines Way, Third Avenue then Elizabeth Way. The ground can be seen ahead of you at the Roydon Road roundabout. Go straight over the roundabout and the entrance to the ground is on the left.

HEYBRIDGE SWIFTS FC

Founded: 1882
Former Names: Heybridge FC
Nickname: 'The Swifts'
Ground: Scraley Road, Heybridge, Maldon, Essex, CM9 8JA
Record Attendance: 2,500 (1996/97)

Colours: Black and White striped shirts, Black shorts
Telephone Nº: (01621) 852978
Ground Capacity: 3,000
Seating Capacity: 550
Web site: www.heybridgeswifts.com

GENERAL INFORMATION
Car Parking: At the ground
Coach Parking: At the ground
Nearest Railway Station: Witham (6 miles)
Nearest Bus Station: Chelmsford
Club Shop: At the ground
Opening Times: Matchdays only
Telephone Nº: –

GROUND INFORMATION
Away Supporters' Entrances & Sections:
No usual segregation

ADMISSION INFO (2011/2012 PRICES)
Adult Standing: £8.00
Adult Seating: £8.00
Child/Concessionary Standing: £4.00
Child/Concessionary Seating: £4.00
Programme Price: £2.00

DISABLED INFORMATION
Wheelchairs: Accommodated
Helpers: Admitted
Prices: Normal prices apply
Disabled Toilets: Yes
Contact: (01621) 852978   (Bookings are not necessary)

Travelling Supporters' Information:
Routes: Take the A414 to Maldon then the B1026 towards Colchester and pass through Heybridge. Turn right at the sign for Tolleshunt Major (Scraley Road) and the ground is on the right; From the M25: Exit the M25 at junction 28 and follow the A12 past Chelmsford. At the end of the 3 lane section (a fair distance) take the B1019 signposted to Hatfield Peverel and Maldon. Follow signs in to Hatfield Peverel village, turning left at the T-junction at the end of the slip road. Pass the Swan pub on the left then turn right towards Maldon and Heybridge opposiute the Duke of Wellington pub. Follow this road for 4 miles through Langford, cross over a bridge then at the large roundabout take first exit to Heybridge. Go straight over the mini roundabout then take the first exit at the next roundabout by the Benbridge Hotel. Pass a small shopping centre, take the first exit at the next roundabout. Follow the road past playing fields and turn right into Scraley Road for the ground.

ILFORD FC

Founded: 1880 (Re-formed in 1987)
Former Names: None
Nickname: 'The Foxes'
Ground: Cricklefield Stadium, 486 High Road, Ilford, IG1 1UE
Record Attendance: 1,632

Colours: Blue & White shirts with Blue shorts
Telephone Nº: (020) 8514-8352
Fax Number: (020) 8514-8352
Ground Capacity: 3,500
Seating Capacity: 216
Web Site: www.ilfordfc.moonfruit.com

GENERAL INFORMATION
Car Parking: At the ground
Coach Parking: At the ground
Nearest Railway Station: Seven Kings (¼ mile)
Nearest Tube Station: Newbury Park (1¾ miles)
Club Shop: None
Opening Times: –
Telephone Nº: –

GROUND INFORMATION
Away Supporters' Entrances & Sections:
No usual segregation

ADMISSION INFO (2011/2012 PRICES)
Adult Standing: £8.00
Adult Seating: £8.00
Senior Citizen/Junior Standing: £4.00
Senior Citizen/Junior Seating: £4.00
Programme Price: Included with admission price

DISABLED INFORMATION
Wheelchairs: Accommodated
Helpers: Admitted
Prices: Normal prices apply for the disabled. Helpers pay concessionary prices
Disabled Toilets: Available
Contact: (020) 8514-8352 (Bookings are not necessary)

Travelling Supporters' Information:
Routes: Take the North Circular Road (A406) to Ilford and exit onto the A118 heading east to Ilford Hill. At the top of Ilford Hill, turn right then immediately left at the roundabout into Winston Way. Continue along the dual carriageway to the Eastern Roundabout, take the second exit into High Road and the ground is on the right hand side behind the Fire Station.

LEISTON FC

Founded: 1880
Former Names: None
Nickname: 'The Blues'
Ground: Victory Road, Leiston   IP16 4DQ
Record Attendance: 1,250 (2009/2010 season)
Pitch Size: 112 × 70 yards

Colours: Royal Blue shirts and shorts
Telephone Nº: (01728) 830308
Fax Number: (01728) 833572
Ground Capacity: 2,500
Seating Capacity: 150
Web Site: www.leistonfc.co.uk

GENERAL INFORMATION
Car Parking: At the ground
Coach Parking: At the ground
Nearest Railway Station: Saxmundham (3½ miles)
Nearest Tube Station: Saxmundham
Club Shop: At the ground
Opening Times: Matchdays or by appointment only
Telephone Nº: 07799 435972

GROUND INFORMATION
Away Supporters' Entrances & Sections:
No usual segregation

ADMISSION INFO (2010/2011 PRICES)
Adult Standing: £8.00
Adult Seating: £8.00
Senior Citizen/Junior Standing: £5.00
Senior Citizen/Junior Seating: 8.00
Programme Price: £1.50

DISABLED INFORMATION
Wheelchairs: Accommodated
Helpers: Admitted
Prices: Normal prices apply for the disabled and helpers
Disabled Toilets: Available in the Clubhouse
Contact: 07799 435972   (Bookings are necessary)

Travelling Supporters' Information:
Routes: Leiston is located midway between Lowestoft and Ipswich, about 3½ miles due east of Saxmundham. Take the A12 to Saxmundham then the B1119 road to Leiston. Upon reaching Leiston, continue along the B1119 (Waterloo Avenue) to the junction with the B1069 and turn right along Park Hill. Take the first turning on the left into Victory Road and the ground is located on the right-hand side by the junction with Huntingfield Road.

MALDON & TIPTREE FC

Founded: 1946
Former Names: Maldon Town FC
Nickname: 'The Blues'
Ground: Wallace Binder Ground, Park Drive, Maldon, Essex CM9 5XX
Record Attendance: 1,163 (vs AFC Sudbury, 2003)

Colours: Blue and White shirts and shorts
Telephone Nº: (01621) 853762
Ground Capacity: 2,500
Seating Capacity: 250
Web site: www.maldonandtiptreefc.co.uk

GENERAL INFORMATION
Car Parking: At the ground
Coach Parking: At the ground
Nearest Railway Station: Witham (8 miles)
Club Shop: None
Opening Times: –
Telephone Nº: –

GROUND INFORMATION
Away Supporters' Entrances & Sections:
No usual segregation

ADMISSION INFO (2011/2012 PRICES)
Adult Standing: £8.00
Adult Seating: £8.00
Senior Citizen/Junior Standing: £5.00
Senior Citizen/Junior Seating: £5.00
Programme Price: £1.00

DISABLED INFORMATION
Wheelchairs: Accommodated
Helpers: Admitted
Prices: Concessionary prices apply for disabled and helpers
Disabled Toilets: Available
Contact: (01621) 853762 (Bookings are not necessary)

Travelling Supporters' Information:
Routes: Exit the M25 at Junction 28 and travel north up the A12. Take the A414 off the A12 signposted for Maldon, follow the A414 into Maldon until you come to Safeways roundabout, turn right, go straight on over the next two roundabouts and the Club is on the right.

NEEDHAM MARKET FC

Founded: 1919
Former Names: None
Nickname: 'The Marketmen'
Ground: Bloomfields, Quinton Road, Needham Market IP6 8DA
Record Attendance: 1,275 (29th March 2008)

Colours: Red shirts with Black shorts and Red socks
Telephone Nº: (01449) 721000
Ground Capacity: 2,000
Seating Capacity: 200
Web Site: www.needhammarketfc.co.uk

GENERAL INFORMATION
Car Parking: At the ground
Coach Parking: At the ground
Nearest Railway Station: Needham Market (½ mile)
Club Shop: Via the club's web site only
Opening Times: –
Telephone Nº: –

GROUND INFORMATION
Away Supporters' Entrances & Sections:
No segregation

ADMISSION INFO (2011/2012 PRICES)
Adult Standing: £8.00
Adult Seating: £8.00
Concessionary Standing: £5.00
Concessionary Seating: £5.00
Note: Under-12s are admitted free of charge
Programme Price: £1.00

DISABLED INFORMATION
Wheelchairs: Accommodated
Helpers: Admitted
Prices: Normal prices apply for the disabled and helpers
Disabled Toilets: Available
Contact: (01449) 721000 (Bookings are not necessary)

Travelling Supporters' Information:
Routes: Exit the A14 to the south of Stowmarket and follow the B1078 (Coddenham Road) into Needham Market. Turn left at the junction with the High Street then right into Barking Road. Take the first turn on the right into Chainhouse Road then turn right at the bottom of the road into Quinton Road. The ground is situated on the left hand side after a short distance.

POTTERS BAR TOWN FC

Founded: 1960
Former Names: None
Nickname: 'The Scholars'
Ground: The South Mimms Travel Stadium, Parkfield, Watkins Rise, Potters Bar   EN6 1QB
Record Attendance: 4,000 (1997)

Colours: Red and Blue shirts with Blue shorts
Telephone Nº: (01727) 832234
Ground Capacity: 2,000
Seating Capacity: 150
Web Site: www.pottersbartown.co.uk

GENERAL INFORMATION
Car Parking: At the ground
Coach Parking: At the ground
Nearest Railway Station: Potters Bar (½ mile)
Nearest Tube Station: High Barnet (4 miles)
Club Shop: None
Opening Times: –
Telephone Nº: –

GROUND INFORMATION
Away Supporters' Entrances & Sections:
No usual segregation

ADMISSION INFO (2011/2012 PRICES)
Adult Standing: £8.00
Adult Seating: £8.00
Senior Citizen Standing: £4.00
Senior Citizen Seating: £4.00
Under-16s Standing: Free of charge
Under-16s Seating: Free of charge
Programme Price: £1.50

DISABLED INFORMATION
Wheelchairs: Accommodated
Helpers: Admitted
Prices: Concessionary prices are charged for the disabled and helpers
Disabled Toilets: None
Contact: (01727) 832234   (Bookings are not necessary)

Travelling Supporters' Information:
Routes: Exit the M25 at Junction 24 and take the A111 Southgate Road into Potters Bar. Turn right into the High Street and the ground is situated on the left hand side of the road after 200 yards.

REDBRIDGE FC

Founded: 1934
Former Names: Ford United FC (formed when Brigg Sports FC and Ford Sports FC merged in 1958)
Nickname: 'Motormen'
Ground: Oakside Stadium, Station Road, Barkingside, Ilford, Essex IG6 1NB
Record Attendance: 1,612

Colours: Red and Black striped shirts, Black shorts
Telephone Nº: (020) 8550-3611
Ground Capacity: 3,000
Seating Capacity: 316
Web site: www.redbridgefc.com

GENERAL INFORMATION
Car Parking: At the ground
Coach Parking: At the ground
Nearest Tube Station: Barkingside (Central Line) adjacent
Nearest Bus Station: Ilford
Club Shop: At the ground
Opening Times: Matchdays only
Telephone Nº: (020) 8550-3611

GROUND INFORMATION
Away Supporters' Entrances & Sections:
Segregation only used when required

ADMISSION INFO (2011/2012 PRICES)
Adult Standing/Seating: £5.00
Student/Senior Citizen Standing/Seating: £3.00
Under-16s Standing/Seating: £1.00
Programme Price: £1.50

DISABLED INFORMATION
Wheelchairs: Accommodated
Helpers: Admitted
Prices: Normal prices apply for disabled & helpers
Disabled Toilets: None
Contact: (020) 8550-3611   (Bookings are not necessary)

Travelling Supporters' Information:
Routes: From the North Circular: Take the A12 from Redbridge Roundabout to Gants Hill Cross. Take the 2nd exit at the roundabout onto the A123 Cranbrook Road. Turn right at the traffic lights after Tesco into Tanners Lane, then third left into Craven Gardens. Take the first right into Carlton Drive, go straight on into Station Road, over the railway bridge (on the left as the road splits) then the ground is first right; From the A12 East: Take the first right after Newbury Park Station (traffic lights at McDonald's) into Horn Road. After ¾ mile, turn right into Craven Gardens, first right into Carlton Drive, then as above.
By Underground: Take the Central Line to Barkingside Station. Exit the Station, turn right outside the Station, then right again into Station Road. The ground is over the railway bridge and the first turning on the right.

ROMFORD FC

Romford FC are currently groundsharing with Aveley FC

Founded: 1876
Former Names: None
Nickname: 'The Boro'
Ground: Mill Field, Mill Road, Aveley   RM15 4SJ
Record Attendance: 820

Colours: Blue and Yellow hooped shirts, Blue shorts
Ground Telephone Nº: (01708) 865940
Ground Capacity: 4,000
Seating Capacity: 400
Web Site: www.romfordfc.com

GENERAL INFORMATION
Car Parking: At the ground
Coach Parking: At the ground
Nearest Railway Station: Rainham (2 miles)
Club Shop: None
Opening Times: –
Telephone Nº: –

GROUND INFORMATION
Away Supporters' Entrances & Sections:
No usual segregation

ADMISSION INFO (2011/2012 PRICES)
Adult Standing/Seating: £8.00
Senior Citizen Standing/Seating: £5.00
Under-16s Standing/Seating: £2.00
Note: Under-11s are admitted free of charge
Programme Price: £2.00

DISABLED INFORMATION
Wheelchairs: Accommodated (but no special facilities)
Helpers: Admitted
Prices: Normal prices apply for the disabled and helpers
Disabled Toilets: None at present
Contact: (01708) 865940   (Bookings are not necessary)

Travelling Supporters' Information:
Routes: Exit the M25 at junction 30 and take the Thames Gateway (A13) towards Aveley. Pass under Purfleet Road flyover then take the next slip road onto the A1306. At the first roundabout, take the 3rd exit, pass over the A13 and at the next roundabout continue straight across into New Road. Take the first turn on the right into Sandy Lane (B1335) then turn right at the next roundabout into Mill Road. The ground is on the left hand side of the road.

SOHAM TOWN RANGERS FC

Founded: 1947
Former Names: Soham Town FC
Nickname: 'The Greens'
Ground: Julius Martin Lane, Soham, Ely CB7 5EQ
Record Attendance: 3,000 (1963)
Colours: Shirts and shorts are Green with White trim
Telephone Nº: (01353) 720732
Ground Capacity: 2,000
Seating Capacity: 250
Web Site: www.webteams.co.uk/sohamtownrangersfc

GENERAL INFORMATION
Car Parking: At the ground
Coach Parking: At the ground
Nearest Railway Station: Ely (5 miles)
Club Shop: None
Opening Times: –
Telephone Nº: –

GROUND INFORMATION
Away Supporters' Entrances & Sections:
No usual segregation

ADMISSION INFO (2011/2012 PRICES)
Adult Standing: £7.00
Adult Seating: £7.00
Senior Citizen/Junior Standing: £4.00
Senior Citizen/Junior Seating: £4.00
Programme Price: £1.50

DISABLED INFORMATION
Wheelchairs: Accommodated
Helpers: Admitted
Prices: Normal prices apply for the disabled and helpers
Disabled Toilets: None
Contact: (01353) 720732 (Bookings are not necessary)

Travelling Supporters' Information:
Routes: Soham is located just to the west of the A142, between Newmarket and Ely. Exit the A142 at the roundabout just to the north of Soham and follow the road named 'The Shade' into town. Continue along this road into Townsend, follow round the bend then turn right into Julius Martin Lane. The ground is on the left hand side towards the end of the lane.

THAMESMEAD TOWN FC

Founded: 1970
Former Names: None
Nickname: 'The Mead'
Ground: Bayliss Avenue, Thamesmead, London, SE28 8NJ
Record Attendance: 400 (1988)

Colours: Green and White shirts with Green shorts
Telephone No: (020) 8311-4211
Fax Number: (020) 8311-4211
Ground Capacity: 400
Seating Capacity: 125
Web Site: www.thamesmeadtownfc.co.uk

GENERAL INFORMATION
Car Parking: At the ground
Coach Parking: None
Nearest Railway Station: Abbey Wood (2 miles)
Club Shop: At the ground
Opening Times: Matchdays only
Telephone No: (020) 8311-4211

GROUND INFORMATION
Away Supporters' Entrances & Sections: No usual segregation

ADMISSION INFO (2011/2012 PRICES)
Adult Standing/Seating: £8.00
Senior Citizen Standing/Seating: £5.00
Under-16s Standing/Seating: £1.00
Programme Price: £1.00

DISABLED INFORMATION
Wheelchairs: Accommodated
Helpers: Admitted
Prices: Normal prices apply for the disabled. Free of charge for helpers
Disabled Toilets: Available
Contact: 07811 254792 (Kellie Discipline – Club Secretary)

Travelling Supporters' Information:
Routes: The ground is located just to the north of the A2016 Eastern Way Road. Exit the Eastern Way at the Carlyle Road interchange, heading north, and turn right at the first roundabout into Crossway. Pass over Crossway Canal and take the next turn on the right into Bayliss Avenue. The ground is situated on the right.

TILBURY FC

Founded: 1900
Former Names: None
Nickname: 'The Dockers'
Ground: Chadfields, St. Chad's Road, Tilbury, RM18 8NL
Record Attendance: 5,500 (1949)

Colours: Black and White striped shirts with Black shorts
Telephone Nº: (01375) 843093
Fax Number: (01375) 859496
Ground Capacity: 4,000
Seating Capacity: 350
Web Site: www.tilburyfc.net

GENERAL INFORMATION
Car Parking: At the ground
Coach Parking: At the ground
Nearest Railway Station: Tilbury Town (1 mile)
Club Shop: None
Opening Times: –
Telephone Nº: –

GROUND INFORMATION
Away Supporters' Entrances & Sections:
No usual segregation

ADMISSION INFO (2011/2012 PRICES)
Adult Standing: £8.00
Adult Seating: £8.00
Senior Citizen/Junior Standing: £5.00
Senior Citizen/Junior Seating: £5.00
Programme Price: £1.50

DISABLED INFORMATION
Wheelchairs: Accommodated
Helpers: Admitted
Prices: Normal prices apply for the disabled and helpers
Disabled Toilets: None
Contact: (01375) 843093 (Bookings are not necessary)

Travelling Supporters' Information:
Routes: Exit the M25 at Junction 30 and take the A13 towards Basildon. After approximately 4 miles, take the A1089 slip road southwards towards Tilbury & the Docks. After a further 2 miles take the slip road signposted for Chadwell St. Mary then turn right at the T-junction onto the A126 Marshfoot Road. Pass the School on the right then take the 3rd exit at the roundabout into St. Chad's Road. After ½ mile take the right hand road fork then take the first turning on the right into Chadfields for the ground.

WALTHAM ABBEY FC

Founded: 1944
Former Names: None
Nickname: 'The Abbotts'
Ground: Capershotts, Sewardstone Road, Waltham Abbey EN9 1LU
Record Attendance: 459 (vs Concord Rangers, 2009)

Colours: Green & White hooped shirts, White shorts
Telephone Nº: (01992) 711287
Ground Capacity: 2,000
Seating Capacity: 300
Web Site: www.wafc.net

GENERAL INFORMATION
Car Parking: At the ground
Coach Parking: At the ground
Nearest Railway Station: Waltham Cross (2½ miles)
Nearest Tube Station: Loughton (5½ miles)
Club Shop: None
Opening Times: –
Telephone Nº: –

GROUND INFORMATION
Away Supporters' Entrances & Sections:
No usual segregation

ADMISSION INFO (2011/2012 PRICES)
Adult Standing/Seating: £8.00
Senior Citizen Standing/Seating: £4.00
Under-16s Standing/Seating: £1.00
Programme Price: £2.00

DISABLED INFORMATION
Wheelchairs: Accommodated
Helpers: Admitted
Prices: Normal prices apply for the disabled and helpers
Disabled Toilets: Planned to be available towards the end of the 2010/2011 season
Contact: (01992) 711287   (Bookings are not necessary)

Travelling Supporters' Information:
Routes: Exit the M25 at Junction 25 and follow the A121 Dowding Way westwards and take the 3rd exit at Sewardstone Roundabout into Sewardstone Road. Pass over the M25 and turn immediately right before the Cemetery for the ground. If you pass a Nissan Garage, you have gone too far!

WALTHAM FOREST FC

Waltham Forest FC are groundsharing with Ilford FC during the 2011/2012 season.

Founded: 1995
Former Names: Leyton Pennant FC (following the merger of Walthamstow Pennant FC and Leyton FC). Walthamstow Pennant were previously Pennant FC.
Nickname: 'The Stags'
Ground: Cricklefield Stadium, 486 High Road, Ilford, IG1 1UE
Record Attendance: 676 (10th February 1996)

Colours: White and Green shirts with White shorts
Ground Telephone Nº: (020) 8530-4551
Fax Number: (020) 8514-8352
Ground Capacity: 3,500
Seating Capacity: 216
Web Site: www.walthamforest-fc.co.uk

GENERAL INFORMATION
Car Parking: At the ground
Coach Parking: At the ground
Nearest Railway Station: Seven Kings (¼ mile)
Nearest Tube Station: Newbury Park (1¾ miles)
Club Shop: None
Opening Times: –
Telephone Nº: –

GROUND INFORMATION
Away Supporters' Entrances & Sections:
No usual segregation

ADMISSION INFO (2011/2012 PRICES)
Adult Standing/Seating: £8.00
Senior Citizen Standing/Seating: £4.00
Junior Standing/Seating: £1.00
Programme Price: £1.50

DISABLED INFORMATION
Wheelchairs: Accommodated
Helpers: Admitted
Prices: Normal prices apply for the disabled and helpers
Disabled Toilets: Available
Contact: – (Bookings are not necessary)

Travelling Supporters' Information:
Routes: Take the North Circular Road (A406) to Ilford and exit onto the A118 heading east to Ilford Hill. At the top of Ilford Hill, turn right then immediately left at the roundabout into Winston Way. Continue along the dual carriageway to the Eastern Roundabout, take the second exit into High Road and the ground is on the right hand side behind the Fire Station.

WARE FC

Founded: 1892
Former Names: Ware Town FC
Nickname: 'The Blues'
Ground: Wodson Park, Wadesmill Road, Ware, SG12 0UQ
Record Attendance: 2,123 (2007)

Colours: Blue shirts with White piping, Blue shorts
Telephone N°: (01920) 462064
Fax Number: (01920) 462565
Ground Capacity: 3,500
Seating Capacity: 500
Web Site: www.ware-fc.co.uk

GENERAL INFORMATION
Car Parking: Ample space available at the ground
Coach Parking: At the ground
Nearest Railway Station: Ware (1½ miles)
Club Shop: At the ground
Opening Times: Matchdays only
Telephone N°: (01920) 462064

GROUND INFORMATION
Away Supporters' Entrances & Sections:
No usual segregation

ADMISSION INFO (2011/2012 PRICES)
Adult Standing: £8.00
Adult Seating: £8.00
Concessionary Standing: £4.00
Concessionary Seating: £4.00
Note: Under-14s are admitted free of charge when accompanying a paying adult
Programme Price: £1.50

DISABLED INFORMATION
Wheelchairs: Accommodated
Helpers: Admitted
Prices: Normal prices apply for the disabled and helpers
Disabled Toilets: Available
Contact: (01920) 462064 (Bookings are not necessary)

Travelling Supporters' Information:
Routes: Take the A10 to the junction with the A1170 to the north of Hertford. Head south on the A1170 (Wadesmill Road) and the ground is on the left almost immediately, just to the north of Ware.

THE RYMAN FOOTBALL LEAGUE DIVISION ONE SOUTH

Secretary Kellie Discipline   **Phone** (01322) 314999

Address The Base, Dartford Business Park, Victoria Road, Dartford DA1 5FS

Web Site www.isthmian.co.uk

Clubs for the 2011/2012 Season

Bognor Regis Town FC	Page 53
Burgess Hill Town FC	Page 54
Chipstead FC	Page 55
Corinthian Casuals FC	Page 56
Crawley Down FC	Page 57
Croydon Athletic FC	Page 58
Dulwich Hamlet FC	Page 59
Eastbourne Town FC	Page 60
Faversham Town FC	Page 61
Folkestone Invicta FC	Page 62
Godalming Town FC	Page 63
Hythe Town FC	Page 64
Maidstone United FC	Page 65
Merstham FC	Page 66
Ramsgate FC	Page 67
Sittingbourne FC	Page 68
Walton & Hersham FC	Page 69
Walton Casuals FC	Page 70
Whitehawk FC	Page 71
Whitstable Town FC	Page 72
Whyteleafe FC	Page 73
Worthing FC	Page 74

BOGNOR REGIS TOWN FC

Founded: 1883
Former Names: None
Nickname: 'The Rocks'
Ground: Nyewood Lane, Bognor Regis PO21 2TY
Record Attendance: 3,642 (1984)
Pitch Size: 116 × 75 yards

Colours: White shirts with Green trim, Green shorts
Telephone Nº: (01243) 822325
Fax Number: (01243) 866151
Ground Capacity: 6,000
Seating Capacity: 250
Web site: www.therocks.co.uk

GENERAL INFORMATION
Supporters Club: David Seabourne, c/o Club
Telephone Nº: (01243) 861336
Car Parking: Outside the ground at the Sports Club
Coach Parking: None
Nearest Railway Station: Bognor Regis (1 mile)
Nearest Bus Station: Bognor Regis (1 mile)
Club Shop: At the ground
Opening Times: Matchdays only
Telephone Nº: (01243) 862045
Police Telephone Nº: (0845) 607-0999

GROUND INFORMATION
Away Supporters' Entrances & Sections:
No usual segregation

ADMISSION INFO (2011/2012 PRICES)
Adult Standing: £8.00
Adult Seating: £9.00
Senior Citizen/Concessionary Standing: £8.00
Senior Citizen/Concessionary Seating: £9.00
Under-18s/Students Standing: £2.50
Under-18s/Students Seating: £2.50
Programme Price: £1.50

DISABLED INFORMATION
Wheelchairs: Accommodated
Helpers: Admitted
Prices: Normal prices apply
Disabled Toilets: Available
Contact: (01243) 822325   (Bookings are not necessary)

Travelling Supporters' Information:
Routes: From the West: Take the M27/A27 to Chichester then the A259 and pass through Bersted towards Bognor Regis. Turn right into Hawthorne Road then left into Nyewood Lane – the ground is on the right; From the East: Take the A27 from Brighton/Worthing and turn left onto the A29 at Fontwell Roundabout. Travel along Shripney Road and turn right at the second roundabout towards Bersted on the A259 then left into Hawthorne Road – then as above.

BURGESS HILL TOWN FC

Founded: 1882
Former Names: None
Nickname: 'The Hillians'
Ground: Leylands Park, Maple Drive, Burgess Hill, RH15 8DL
Record Attendance: 2,005 (vs AFC Wimbledon during the 2004/05 season)

Colours: Yellow and Black shirts with Black shorts
Telephone Nº: (01444) 254832
Ground Capacity: 2,250
Seating Capacity: 307
Web Site: www.bhtfc.co.uk

GENERAL INFORMATION
Car Parking: At the ground
Coach Parking: At the ground
Nearest Railway Station: Wivelsfield (½ mile)
Club Shop: At the ground
Opening Times: Matchdays only, 2.00pm to 5.00pm
Telephone Nº: (01444) 254832

GROUND INFORMATION
Away Supporters' Entrances & Sections:
No usual segregation

ADMISSION INFO (2011/2012 PRICES)
Adult Standing/Seating: £9.00
Senior Citizen/Concessionary Standing/Seating: £6.00
Under-16s Standing/Seating: £2.00
Programme Price: £2.00

DISABLED INFORMATION
Wheelchairs: Accommodated
Helpers: Admitted
Prices: Normal prices apply for the disabled and helpers
Disabled Toilets: None
Contact: (01444) 254832   (Bookings are necessary)

Travelling Supporters' Information:
Routes: Exit the A23 at the junction with the A2300 just to the north of Hickstead show ground. Head east along the A2300, following signs to Burgess Hill/Wivelsfield Station. Go straight on at the first roundabout, then turn left at the second roundabout onto the A273 (past The Triangle Leisure Centre). Take the first exit at the next roundabout then take the 3rd exit at the next roundabout into London Road. Drive up the hill for 300 yards then take the first left into Maple Drive. Leylands Park is on the left hand side of the road after about ¾ mile. Look out for the parking signs and the floodlights.

CHIPSTEAD FC

Founded: 1906
Former Names: None
Nickname: 'Chips'
Ground: High Road, Chipstead   CR5 3SF
Record Attendance: 1,170

Colours: Green & White hooped shirts, Black shorts
Telephone Nº: (01737) 553250
Ground Capacity: 2,000
Seating Capacity: 150
Web Site: www.chipsteadfc.com

GENERAL INFORMATION
Car Parking: At the ground
Coach Parking: At the ground
Nearest Railway Station: Chipstead (1¾ miles)
Club Shop: None
Opening Times: –
Telephone Nº: –

GROUND INFORMATION
Away Supporters' Entrances & Sections:
No usual segregation

ADMISSION INFO (2011/2012 PRICES)
Adult Standing: £8.00
Adult Seating: £8.00
Senior Citizen/Concessionary Standing: £5.00
Senior Citizen/Concessionary Seating: £5.00
Note: Under-16s are admitted free of charge
Programme Price: £1.00

DISABLED INFORMATION
Wheelchairs: Accommodated
Helpers: Admitted
Prices: Concessionary prices are charged for the disabled and helpers
Disabled Toilets: None
Contact: (01737) 553250   (Bookings are not necessary)

Travelling Supporters' Information:
Routes: From the South: Exit the M25 at Junction 7, take M23 signposted Croydon and continue into the A23. After about 1 mile turn left into Star Lane at the traffic lights adjacent to a BP garage.* Follow Star Lane into Elmore Road, keeping the church and the green on the left until reaching the crossroads with High Road. Turn left (signposted Lower Kingswood & Reigate) and parking for away supporters is 200 yards on the left; From Purley/Croydon: Take the A23 southbound towards Coulsdon and take the Coulsdon bypass, signposted M23 and Gatwick. At the second set of lights after the bypass turn right into Star Lane – there is a BP garage on the corner. Then as from * above.

CORINTHIAN-CASUALS FC

Founded: 1882
Former Names: Formed by the amalgamation of Corinthians FC and Casuals FC in 1939
Nickname: 'Casuals'
Ground: King George's Field, Queen Mary Close, Hook Rise South, Tolworth   KT6 7NA
Record Attendance: 1,300 (2004/05 season)

Colours: Chocolate and Pink halved shirts with Navy Blue shorts
Telephone Nº: (020) 8397-3368
Ground Capacity: 2,000
Seating Capacity: 161
Web Site: www.corinthian-casuals.com

GENERAL INFORMATION
Car Parking: At the ground
Coach Parking: At the ground
Nearest Railway Station: Tolworth (¼ mile)
Nearest Tube Station: Morden (5½ miles)
Club Shop: At the ground and on the web site
Opening Times: Matchdays only at the ground
Telephone Nº: –

GROUND INFORMATION
Away Supporters' Entrances & Sections:
No usual segregation

ADMISSION INFO (2011/2012 PRICES)
Adult Standing/Seating: £8.00
Senior Citizen/Student Standing/Seating: £4.00
Under-16s Standing/Seating: £2.00
Note: Under-11s are admitted free of charge
Programme Price: £2.00

DISABLED INFORMATION
Wheelchairs: Accommodated
Helpers: Admitted
Prices: Normal prices apply for the disabled and helpers
Disabled Toilets: Available
Contact: (020) 8397-3368   (Bookings are not necessary)

Travelling Supporters' Information:
Routes: From the South: Exit the M25 Junction 10 and follow the A3 towards London. Continue under the Hook Junction roundabout, move into the left hand then exit for Tolworth Junction. Take the 4th exit at the Tolworth Junction roundabout then almost immediately take the slip road on left onto Hook Rise South. The ground is on the left after ½ mile; From London: Take the A3 then exit at Tolworth Junction exit. Take the 2nd exit at the roundabout then almost immediately take the slip road on the left onto Hook Rise South.   Note: From both directions, please be careful not to miss the slip road into Hook Rise South!

CRAWLEY DOWN FC

Founded: 1983
Former Names: Crawley Down United FC and Crawley Down Village FC
Nickname: 'The Anvils'
Ground: Haven Sportsfield, Haven Centre, Hophurst Lane, Crawley Down RH10 4LJ
Pitch Size: 110 × 72 yards

Record Attendance: 404 (during 1996)
Colours: Red shirts and shorts
Telephone Nº: –
Ground Capacity: 1,000
Seating Capacity: –
Web Site: www.crawleydownfc.com
E-mail contact: crawleydownfc@btinternet.com

GENERAL INFORMATION

Car Parking: Ample spaces at the ground
Coach Parking: At the ground
Nearest Railway Station: East Grinstead (2½ miles)
Club Shop: None
Opening Times: –
Telephone Nº: –

GROUND INFORMATION

Away Supporters' Entrances & Sections:
No usual segregation

ADMISSION INFO (2010/2011 PRICES)

Adult Standing: £8.00
Adult Seating: £8.00
Senior Citizen/Junior Standing: £6.00
Senior Citizen/Junior Seating: £6.00
Note: 'Junior Anvils' are admitted free of charge
Programme Price: £1.50

DISABLED INFORMATION

Wheelchairs: Accommodated
Helpers: Admitted
Prices: Normal prices apply for the disabled and helpers
Disabled Toilets: Available
Contact: – (Bookings are not necessary)

Travelling Supporters' Information:

Routes: From the North & West: Exit the M23 at Junction 10 and take the A264 towards East Grinstead. Take the 2nd exit at the roundabout by the Copthorne Hotel then take the 3rd exit at the next roundabout onto the B2028 heading southwards towards Turners Hill. After approximately 1 mile, turn left into Sandy Lane, continue to the end of the road and turn left by the war memorial towards Felbridge. The Haven Centre is on the left after a couple of bends in the road; From the East: Travel through East Grinstead on the A22 until the junction with the A264 at the Felbridge traffic lights. Turn left (signposted for Crawley) then take the left fork towards Crawley Down. The Haven Centre is on the right after approximately 1½ miles; From the South: Travel through Turners Hill heading northwards on the B2028 and after approximately 2 miles take the second turning on the right into Vicarage Road. Continue along Vicarage Road into Hophurst Lane and the Haven Centre is on the left.

CROYDON ATHLETIC FC

Founded: 1947
Former Names: Norwood FC (founded 1947) and Wandsworth FC (founded 1948) amalgamated to form Wandsworth & Norwood FC in 1986. The club was renamed Croydon Athletic FC in 1990
Nickname: 'The Rams'
Ground: The Keith Tuckey Stadium, Mayfield Road, Thornton Heath   CR7 6DN

Record Attendance: 1,372 (2004/05 season)
Colours: Maroon shirts and shorts
Telephone N°: 07752 926809
Ground Capacity: 3,000
Seating Capacity: 163
Web Site: www.croydonathletic.net

GENERAL INFORMATION
Car Parking: At the ground
Coach Parking: At the ground
Nearest Railway Station: Norbury (1 mile)
Club Shop: In the Clubhouse
Opening Times: Matchdays only
Telephone N°: 07752 926809

GROUND INFORMATION
Away Supporters' Entrances & Sections:
No usual segregation

ADMISSION INFO (2011/2012 PRICES)
Adult Standing/Seating: £8.00
Senior Citizen/Student Standing/Seating: £4.00
Under-16s Standing/Seating: Free of charge
Programme Price: £2.00

DISABLED INFORMATION
Wheelchairs: Accommodated
Helpers: Admitted
Prices: Normal prices apply for the disabled and helpers
Disabled Toilets: Available
Contact: 07752 926809   (Bookings are not necessary)

Travelling Supporters' Information:
Routes: From the North: Take the A23 London Road to the roundabout at Thornton Heath and continue along the A23 Thornton Road. Take the second right into Silverleigh Road, fork left after 50 yards (signposted Croydon Athletic FC) into Trafford Road then continue into Mayfield Road. Turn left after the last house then follow the lane past the allotments for the ground; From Croydon: Travel up the A235 London Road, turn left at the roundabout then right into Silverleigh Road. Then as above.

DULWICH HAMLET FC

Founded: 1893
Former Names: None
Nickname: 'The Hamlet'
Ground: Champion Hill Stadium, Edgar Kail Way, London SE22 8BD
Record Attendance: 1,835 (14th November 1998)
Pitch Size: 110 × 70 yards

Colours: Pink and Navy Blue quartered shirts with Navy Blue shorts
Telephone Nº: (0207) 274-8707
Daytime Phone Nº: (0207) 274-8707
Fax Number: (0207) 501-9255
Ground Capacity: 3,000
Seating Capacity: 500
Web site: www.dulwichhamletfc.co.uk

GENERAL INFORMATION
Car Parking: 50 spaces available at the ground
Coach Parking: At the ground
Nearest Railway Station: East Dulwich (adjacent)
Nearest Tube Station: Brixton (3½ miles)
Club Shop: At the ground
Opening Times: Matchdays only
Telephone Nº: (0207) 274-8707

GROUND INFORMATION
Away Supporters' Entrances & Sections: No usual segregation

ADMISSION INFO (2011/2012 PRICES)
Adult Standing: £8.00
Adult Seating: £8.00
Concessionary Standing: £4.00
Concessionary Seating: £4.00
Note: Under-12s are admitted free of charge when accompanying a paying adult
Programme Price: £1.50

DISABLED INFORMATION
Wheelchairs: 10 spaces available in the front of the Main Stand
Helpers: Admitted
Prices: Please phone the club for information
Disabled Toilets: Available behind the disabled area
Contact: (0207) 274-8707 (Bookings are necessary)

Travelling Supporters' Information:
Routes: From the Elephant & Castle: Go down Walworth Road, through Camberwell's one-way system and along Denmark Hill. Turn left by the railway into Champion Park and then right at the end down Grave Lane to the ground in Dog Kennel Hill; From the South: Come up through Streatham on the A23, turn right to Tulse Hill along the A205 (Christchurch Road) and carry on towards Sydenham. Turn left at The Grove into Lordship Lane and carry on to East Dulwich.

EASTBOURNE TOWN FC

Founded: 1881
Former Names: Devonshire Park FC
Nickname: 'Town'
Ground: The Saffrons, Compton Place Road, Eastbourne BN21 1EA
Record Attendance: 7,378 (1953)

Colours: Yellow shirts with Blue shorts
Telephone Nº: (01323) 723734
Ground Capacity: 3,000
Seating Capacity: 200
Web Site: www.eastbournetownfc.com

GENERAL INFORMATION
Car Parking: At the ground
Coach Parking: At the ground
Nearest Railway Station: Eastbourne (½ mile)
Club Shop: None
Opening Times: –
Telephone Nº: –

GROUND INFORMATION
Away Supporters' Entrances & Sections: No usual segregation

ADMISSION INFO (2011/2012 PRICES)
Adult Standing: £8.00
Adult Seating: £8.00
Senior Citizen Standing: £3.00
Senior Citizen Seating: £3.00
Under-16s Standing: £1.00
Under-16s Seating: £1.00
Programme Price: £1.50

DISABLED INFORMATION
Wheelchairs: Accommodated
Helpers: Admitted
Prices: Normal prices apply for the disabled and helpers
Disabled Toilets: None
Contact: (01323) 723734   (Bookings are not necessary)

Travelling Supporters' Information:
Routes: Take the A22 to Eastbourne and, at the Polegate Roundabout, take the A27 before joining the A2270 Eastbourne Road. Take the second exit at the roundabout into Willingdon Road (still A2270) and continue before turning right at the mini-roundabout next to Eastbourne Railway station to turn into Grove Road. Continue past the council offices into Meads Road then turn right into Compton Place Road. The ground is located on the right hand side of the road.

FAVERSHAM TOWN FC

Founded: 1884
Former Names: None
Nickname: 'The Lilywhites'
Ground: Salters Lane, Faversham   ME13 8ND
Record Attendance: Not known
Colours: White shirts with Black shorts
Telephone Nº: (01795) 591900
Ground Capacity: 2,000
Seating Capacity: 200
Web Site: www.favershamtownfc.co.uk

GENERAL INFORMATION
Car Parking: At the ground
Coach Parking: At the ground
Nearest Railway Station: Faversham (¼ mile)
Club Shop: None
Opening Times: –
Telephone Nº: –

GROUND INFORMATION
Away Supporters' Entrances & Sections:
No usual segregation

ADMISSION INFO (2011/2012 PRICES)
Adult Standing: £8.00
Adult Seating: £8.00
Senior Citizen/Under-18s Standing: £4.00
Senior Citizen/Under-18s Seating: £4.00
Under-16s Standing/Seating: £1.00
Note: Children aged 5 and under are admitted free of charge

DISABLED INFORMATION
Wheelchairs: Accommodated
Helpers: Admitted
Prices: Normal prices apply for the disabled and helpers
Disabled Toilets: Please contact the club for details
Contact: (01795) 591900   (Bookings are necessary)

Travelling Supporters' Information:
Routes: Exit the M2 at Junction 6 and follow the A251 (Ashford Road) north into Faversham. Turn right at the junction with the A2 into Canterbury Road then right again into Salters Lane for the ground.

FOLKESTONE INVICTA FC

Founded: 1936
Former Names: None
Nickname: 'The Seasiders'
Ground: Buzzlines Stadium, Cheriton Road, Folkestone, Kent   CT19 5JU
Record Attendance: 7,881 (1958)

Ground Capacity: 6,250
Seating Capacity: 900
Colours: Amber and Black striped shirts with Black shorts and socks
Telephone Nº: (01303) 257461
Web site: www.folkestoneinvicta.co.uk

GENERAL INFORMATION
Car Parking: Street parking
Coach Parking: At the ground
Nearest Railway Station: Folkestone Central and Folkestone West
Club Shop: At the ground
Opening Times: Matchdays only
Telephone Nº: (01303) 257266

GROUND INFORMATION
Away Supporters' Entrances & Sections:
No usual segregation

ADMISSION INFO (2011/2012 PRICES)
Adult Standing: £8.00
Adult Seating: £8.00
Senior Citizen Standing/Seating: £4.00
Under-16s Standing/Seating: £2.00
Note: Under-16s are admitted free of charge when accompanying a paying adult
Programme Price: £2.00

DISABLED INFORMATION
Wheelchairs: Accommodated
Helpers: Admitted
Prices: Normal prices apply for disabled & helpers
Disabled Toilets: Available in the Clubhouse (ramped access)
Contact: (01303) 257461   (Bookings are not necessary)

Travelling Supporters' Information:
Routes: Exit the M20 at Junction 13, head south on the A20 for ½ mile and at the traffic lights turn left onto the A2034. The ground is about ¼ mile along towards the Morrisons Foodstore on the left-hand side of the road. Parking is available in front of the Stripes Club or the Cricket Ground.

GODALMING TOWN FC

Founded: 1979
Former Names: None
Nickname: 'The Gs'
Ground: Wey Court, Meadrow, Godalming, GU7 3JE
Record Attendance: 1,305 (2002)
Colours: Yellow shirts with Green shorts
Telephone Nº: (01483) 417520
Ground Capacity: 3,000
Seating Capacity: 200
Web Site: www.godalmingtownfc.co.uk

GENERAL INFORMATION
Car Parking: A public car park is adjacent to the ground
Coach Parking: A public car park is adjacent
Nearest Railway Station: Farncombe (½ mile)
Club Shop: At the ground
Opening Times: Matchdays only. Also online sales.
Telephone Nº: –

GROUND INFORMATION
Away Supporters' Entrances & Sections:
No usual segregation

ADMISSION INFO (2011/2012 PRICES)
Adult Standing/Seating: £8.00
Senior Citizen Standing/Seating: £4.00
Under-16s Standing/Seating: £1.00
Note: Under-11s are admitted free of charge when accompanied by a paying adult
Programme Price: £1.50

DISABLED INFORMATION
Wheelchairs: Accommodated
Helpers: Admitted
Prices: Normal prices apply for the disabled and helpers
Disabled Toilets: None
Contact: (01483) 417520   (Bookings are not necessary)

Travelling Supporters' Information:
Routes: From Guildford, take the A3100 towards Godalming. After passing the Manor Inn on the left then the petrol station on the right. Wey Court is on the right hand side of the road after a further 50 yards; From Godalming, head towards Guildford on the A3100. Pass the Three Lions pub on the left then turn left into Wey Court immediately after the Leathern Bottle pub.

HYTHE TOWN FC

Founded: 1910
Former Names: None
Nickname: 'Town'
Ground: Reachfields Stadium, Fort Road, Hythe, CT21 6JS
Record Attendance: 2,147 (during 1990)
Pitch Size: 110 × 72 yards
Colours: Red shirts with White panels & sleeves and Red shorts
Telephone Nº: (01303) 238256
Clubhouse Number: (01303) 264932
Ground Capacity: 3,000
Seating Capacity: 300 approximately
Web Site: www.hythetownfc.co.uk

GENERAL INFORMATION
Car Parking: At the ground
Coach Parking: At the ground (Contact the club)
Nearest Railway Station: Sandling (1½ miles)
Nearest Bus Station: Hythe (½ mile)
Club Shop: None, but souvenirs and programmes are sold at the bar in the Clubhouse
Opening Times: –
Telephone Nº: –

GROUND INFORMATION
Away Supporters' Entrances & Sections:
No usual segregation

ADMISSION INFO (2010/2011 PRICES)
Adult Standing: £7.50
Adult Seating: £7.50
Senior Citizen/Concessionary Standing: £4.00
Senior Citizen/Concessionary Seating: £4.00
Under-15s Standing/Seating: £2.00
Programme Price: £1.00 (50p if bought with admission)

DISABLED INFORMATION
Wheelchairs: Accommodated
Helpers: Admitted
Prices: Normal prices apply for the disabled and helpers
Disabled Toilets: Available
Contact: (01303) 264932 (Bookings are not necessary)

Travelling Supporters' Information:
Routes: From the North: Exit the M20 at Junction 11 and follow the A20 southwards. At Newingreen, turn left onto the A261 and follow into Hythe then carry straight on at the traffic lights into Scanlons Bridge Road (A2008). Turn right at the traffic lights onto the A259 Dymchurch Road then first left into Fort Road for the ground; From the East or West: Take the A259 into Hythe and turn into Fort Road which is to the south of the A259.

MAIDSTONE UNITED FC

Maidstone United FC are groundsharing with Sittingbourne FC during the 2011/2012 season.

Founded: 1992
Former Names: Maidstone Invicta FC
Nickname: 'The Stones'
Ground: Bourne Park, Central Park Complex, Eurolink, Sittingbourne ME10 3SB
Record Attendance: 1,589 (at Ashford)

Colours: Amber shirts with Black shorts
Telephone Nº: (01233) 611838
Ground Capacity: 3,000
Seating Capacity: 300
Web Site: www.maidstoneunited.co.uk

GENERAL INFORMATION
Car Parking: Ample spaces available at the ground
Coach Parking: Ample spaces available at the ground
Nearest Railway Station: Sittingbourne (1½ miles)
Club Shop: None
Opening Times: –
Telephone Nº: –

GROUND INFORMATION
Away Supporters' Entrances & Sections:
No usual segregation

ADMISSION INFO (2011/2012 PRICES)
Adult Standing/Seating: 10.00
Senior Citizen/Student Standing/Seating: £7.00
Under-17s Standing/Seating: £4.00
Under-11s: Admitted free of charge with a paying adult
Programme Price: £2.00

DISABLED INFORMATION
Wheelchairs: Accommodated
Helpers: Admitted
Prices: Normal prices apply for the disabled. Free for helpers
Disabled Toilets: Available
Contact: (01233) 611838   (Bookings are not necessary)

Travelling Supporters' Information:
Routes: Exit the M2 at junction 5, take the A249 towards Sittingbourne. Bear left at the first slip road and take the A2 towards Sittingbourne Town Centre. Follow the A2 into the one way system and follow directions to Canterbury (NOT the town centre) until you reach a roundabout next to the Railway station. Take the third exit in St. Michael's Road (still the A2), pass the fire station on your left and turn left into Crown Quay Lane at the first set of traffic lights. Pass under the railway bridge then turn right into Eurolink Way at the roundabout, bear left into Castle Road and continue ahead (do not turn into Dolphin Road). Take the third exit at the small roundabout into Stadium Way, turn right into Church Road the left into the football club car park.

MERSTHAM FC

Founded: 1905
Former Names: None
Nickname: 'The Moatsiders'
Ground: Moatside Stadium, Weldon Way, Merstham RH1 3QB
Record Attendance: 1,587 (9th November 2002)
Colours: Amber & Black striped shirts, Black shorts
Telephone Nº: (01737) 644046
Fax Number: (01737) 644046
Ground Capacity: 2,500
Seating Capacity: 174
Web Site: www.mersthamfc.co.uk

GENERAL INFORMATION
Car Parking: At the ground
Coach Parking: At the ground
Nearest Railway Station: Merstham (½ mile)
Club Shop: At the ground
Opening Times: Matchdays only from 1 hour before kick-off
Telephone Nº: (01737) 644046

GROUND INFORMATION
Away Supporters' Entrances & Sections:
No usual segregation

ADMISSION INFO (2011/2012 PRICES)
Adult Standing: £8.00
Adult Seating: £8.00
Concessionary Standing: £5.00
Concessionary Seating: £5.00
Programme Price: £1.50

DISABLED INFORMATION
Wheelchairs: Accommodated
Helpers: Admitted
Prices: Normal prices apply for the disabled and helpers
Disabled Toilets: Available
Contact: (01737) 644046   (Bookings are not necessary)

Travelling Supporters' Information:
Routes: From the North: Take the A23 to Merstham. After entering Merstham, pass the Feathers Public House in the High Street, look for the brown tourist sign and leave Merstham village by turning left down School Hill, continuing into Bletchingley Road. Take the 5th turn on the right for Weldon Way. The Clubhouse and a small car park are on the right after a short distance; From the South: Take the A23 to Merstham, look for the brown tourist information sign then take the first turn on the right down School Hill into Bletchinley Road. Take the 5th turn on the right for Weldon Way and the Moatside Stadium.

RAMSGATE FC

Founded: 1945
Former Names: Ramsgate Athletic FC
Nickname: 'The Rams' or 'The Redskins'
Ground: Southwood Stadium, Prices Avenue, Ramsgate CT11 0AN
Record Attendance: 5,200 vs Margate (1956/57)
Pitch Size: 112 × 74 yards

Colours: Red shirts and shorts
Telephone N°: (01843) 591662
Fax Number: (01843) 591662
Ground Capacity: 2,500
Seating Capacity: 340
Web site: www.ramsgate-fc.co.uk

GENERAL INFORMATION
Car Parking: 50 spaces available at the ground
Coach Parking: At the ground
Nearest Railway Station: Ramsgate (10 minutes walk)
Nearest Bus Station: Ramsgate
Club Shop: At the ground
Opening Times: Matchdays only
Telephone N°: (01843) 591662

GROUND INFORMATION
Away Supporters' Entrances & Sections:
No usual segregation

ADMISSION INFO (2011/2012 PRICES)
Adult Standing/Seating: £8.00
Under-17s Standing/Seating: £2.50
Senior Citizen/Concessionary Standing/Seating: £5.00
Under-12s: Admitted free of charge with a paying adult
Programme Price: £2.00

DISABLED INFORMATION
Wheelchairs: Accommodated
Helpers: Admitted
Prices: Normal prices apply for the disabled and helpers
Disabled Toilets: Available in the Clubhouse
Contact: (01843) 591662   (Bookings are not necessary)

Travelling Supporters' Information:
Routes: Approach Ramsgate via A299 (Canterbury/London) or A256 (Dover/Folkestone) to Lord of Manor roundabout. Follow the signs to Ramsgate along Canterbury Road East, take 2nd exit at the 1st roundabout then the 2nd exit at the next roundabout into London Road. Take the 3rd turning on the left into St Mildred's Road, then 1st left into Queen Bertha Road. After a right hand bend, turn left into Southwood Road and the 1st left into Prices Avenue. The stadium is at the end of Prices Avenue.

SITTINGBOURNE FC

Founded: 1886
Former Names: Sittingbourne United FC
Nickname: 'The Brickies'
Ground: Bourne Park, Central Park Complex, Eurolink, Sittingbourne ME10 3SB
Record Attendance: 5,951 (26th January 1993)

Colours: Red and Black striped shirts with Black shorts
Telephone Nº: (01795) 435077
Ground Capacity: 3,000
Seating Capacity: 300
Web Site: www.sittingbournefc.co.uk
E-mail: bournefc@hotmail.com

GENERAL INFORMATION
Car Parking: Ample spaces available at the ground
Coach Parking: Ample spaces available at the ground
Nearest Railway Station: Sittingbourne (1½ miles)
Club Shop: At the ground
Opening Times: During matches only
Telephone Nº: 0792 904-5457

GROUND INFORMATION
Away Supporters' Entrances & Sections:
No usual segregation

ADMISSION INFO (2011/2012 PRICES)
Adult Standing/Seating: £8.00
Concessionary Standing/Seating: £4.00
Under-16s Standing/Seating: £3.00
Note: Under-5s are admitted free of charge
Programme Price: £1.50

DISABLED INFORMATION
Wheelchairs: Accommodated
Helpers: Admitted
Prices: Normal prices apply for the disabled and helpers
Disabled Toilets: Available
Contact: (01795) 435077 (Bookings are not necessary)

Travelling Supporters' Information:
Routes: Exit the M2 at junction 5, take the A249 towards Sittingbourne. Bear left at the first slip road and take the A2 towards Sittingbourne Town Centre. Follow the A2 into the one way system and follow directions to Canterbury (NOT the town centre) until you reach a roundabout next to the Railway station. Take the third exit in St. Michael's Road (still the A2), pass the fire station on your left and turn left into Crown Quay Lane at the first set of traffic lights. Pass under the railway bridge then turn right into Eurolink Way at the roundabout, bear left into Castle Road and continue ahead (do not turn into Dolphin Road). Take the third exit at the small roundabout into Stadium Way, turn right into Church Road the left into the football club car park.

WALTON & HERSHAM FC

Founded: 1896
Former Names: None
Nickname: 'The Swans'
Ground: Sports Ground, Stompond Lane, Walton-on-Thames, Surrey KT12 1HF
Record Attendance: 10,300 (vs Crook Town 1/3/52)
Pitch Size: 110 × 70 yards

Colours: Shirts and shorts are Red with White trim
Telephone Nº: (01932) 245263 (Boardroom)
Contact Phone Nº: (01932) 244967 (Clubhouse)
Ground Capacity: 5,000
Seating Capacity: 400
Web site: www.waltonandhershamfc.org.uk

GENERAL INFORMATION
Car Parking: 200 spaces available at the ground
Coach Parking: At the ground
Nearest Railway Station: Walton-on-Thames (¾ mile)
Nearest Tube Station: Heathrow Terminal 4 (8 miles)
Club Shop: At the ground
Opening Times: Matchdays only

GROUND INFORMATION
Away Supporters' Entrances & Sections:
No usual segregation

ADMISSION INFO (2011/2012 PRICES)
Adult Standing: £8.00
Adult Seating: £9.00
Concessionary Standing: £5.00
Concessionary Standing: £5.00
Programme Price: £1.50

DISABLED INFORMATION
Wheelchairs: Accommodated
Helpers: Please phone the club for information
Prices: Please phone the club for information
Disabled Toilets: None
Contact: (01932) 245263 (Bookings are not necessary)

Travelling Supporters' Information:
Routes: From the South: Exit the M25 at Junction 10 and take the A3 to London. After a short distance, turn left onto the A245 and at the traffic lights turn right into Seven Hills Road (B365). Proceed for approximately 2 miles and at the 2nd roundabout take the 2nd exit. At the next roundabout take the 1st exit and at the next roundabout, the 3rd turn-off into Stompond Lane. The car/coach park is approximately 150 yards on the right hand side; From the North: Take the M25 then follow the M3 towards London. At Junction 1 take the A308 towards Staines then turn left on to the A244 at the traffic lights. Continue along the A244 crossing the Thames at Walton Bridge, stay in the middle lane and continue into New Zealand Avenue (still A244). Continue on the A244 into Hersham Road then turn right at the mini-roundabout into Stompond Lane for the ground.

WALTON CASUALS FC

Founded: 1948
Former Names: None
Nickname: 'The Stags'
Ground: The Waterside Stadium, Waterside Drive, Walton-on-Thames KT12 2JG
Record Attendance: 1,748 (12th April 2004)
Colours: Tangerine shirts with Black shorts
Telephone Nº: (01932) 787749
Ground Capacity: 2,000
Seating Capacity: 153
Web Site: www.waltoncasualsfc.co.uk

GENERAL INFORMATION
Car Parking: At the ground
Coach Parking: At the ground
Nearest Railway Station: Upper Halliford (3¾ miles)
Club Shop: At the ground
Opening Times: Matchdays only from 1 hour before kick-off
Telephone Nº: –

GROUND INFORMATION
Away Supporters' Entrances & Sections:
No usual segregation

ADMISSION INFO (2011/2012 PRICES)
Adult Standing/Seating: £8.00
Senior Citizen Standing/Seating: £5.00
Junior Standing/Seating: £2.00
Note: Under-12s are admitted free of charge
Programme Price: £2.00

DISABLED INFORMATION
Wheelchairs: Accommodated
Helpers: Admitted
Prices: Normal prices apply for the disabled and helpers
Disabled Toilets: Available
Contact: (01932) 787749   (Bookings are not necessary)

Travelling Supporters' Information:
Routes: From the South: Take the A3, exit at the Esher turn-off onto the A309 and follow until the Scilly Isles Roundabout, turning right onto Hampton Court Way (still the A309). Just before Hampton Court Bridge turn left onto Hurst Road (A3050), follow for approximately 3½ miles then turn right into Waterside Drive for the ground.

WHITEHAWK FC

Founded: 1945
Former Names: Whitehawk & Manor Farm Old Boys
Nickname: 'The Hawks'
Ground: The Enclosed Ground, East Brighton Park, Brighton   BN2 5TS
Record Attendance: 2,100 (1988/89 season)

Colours: Red shirts and shorts
Telephone Nº: (01273) 609736
Ground Capacity: 3,000
Seating Capacity: 200
Web Site: www.whitehawkfc.co.uk

GENERAL INFORMATION
Car Parking: At the ground
Coach Parking: At the ground
Nearest Railway Station: London Road (3¼ miles)
Club Shop: None
Opening Times: –
Telephone Nº: –

GROUND INFORMATION
Away Supporters' Entrances & Sections:
No usual segregation

ADMISSION INFO (2011/2012 PRICES)
Adult Standing: £5.00
Adult Seating: £5.00
Concessionary Standing: £3.00
Concessionary Seating: £3.00
Under-16s Standing/Seating: Free of charge
Programme Price: Included with admission

DISABLED INFORMATION
Wheelchairs: Accommodated
Helpers: Admitted
Prices: Concessionary prices are charged for the disabled and helpers
Disabled Toilets: None
Contact: (01273) 609736   (Bookings are not necessary)

Travelling Supporters' Information:
Routes: Take the M23/A23 to the junction with the A27 on the outskirts of Brighton then follow the A27 towards Lewes. After passing Sussex University on the left, take the slip road onto the B2123 (signposted Falmer, Rottingdean) and continue for approximately 2 miles before turning right at the traffic lights into Warren Road by the Downs Hotel. Continue for approximately 1 mile then turn left at the traffic lights into Wilson Avenue. After 1¼ miles, turn left at the foot of the hill into East Brighton Park.

WHITSTABLE TOWN FC

Founded: 1886
Former Names: None
Nickname: 'The Oystermen'
Ground: The KRBS.com Belmont Ground, Belmont Road, Whitstable   CT5 1QP
Record Attendance: 2,500 (19th October 1987)

Colours: Red and White shirts with White shorts
Telephone Nº: (01227) 266012
Ground Capacity: 2,000
Seating Capacity: 500
Web Site: www.whitstabletownfc.co.uk

GENERAL INFORMATION
Car Parking: At the ground
Coach Parking: At the ground (Please book in advance)
Nearest Railway Station: Whitstable (½ mile)
Club Shop: None
Opening Times: –
Telephone Nº: –

GROUND INFORMATION
Away Supporters' Entrances & Sections: No usual segregation

ADMISSION INFO (2011/2012 PRICES)
Adult Standing/Seating: £8.00
Concessionary Standing/Seating: 4.00
Under-16s Standing/Seating: £1.00
Programme Price: £1.40

DISABLED INFORMATION
Wheelchairs: Accommodated
Helpers: Admitted
Prices: Concessionary prices are charged for the disabled. Helpers are admitted free of charge
Disabled Toilets: Available
Contact: (01227) 266012   (Bookings are not necessary)

Travelling Supporters' Information:
Routes: Exit the M2 at Junction 7 and follow the A299 towards Margate. Exit the A299 at Clapham Hill and follow the A290 (Borstal Hill) into Whitstable. Continue along the A290 (which becomes Canterbury Road) then turn right into Belmont Road just before the railway line. Continue along Belmont Road, past the cricket ground, turn right into Millstrood Road then right again into Grimshall Road. The entrance to the Belmont Ground is on the right after approximately 300 yards.

WHYTELEAFE FC

Founded: 1946
Former Names: None
Nickname: 'The Leafe'
Ground: 15 Church Road, Whyteleafe CR3 0AR
Record Attendance: 2,617 (2004/05 season)

Colours: Green shirts with Black shorts
Telephone Nº: (020) 8660-5491
Fax Number: (020) 8645-0422
Ground Capacity: 5,000
Seating Capacity: 400
Web Site: www.theleafe.co.uk

GENERAL INFORMATION
Car Parking: Street parking only
Coach Parking: Street parking only
Nearest Railway Station: Whyteleafe South (¼ mile)
Club Shop: At the ground
Opening Times: Matchdays only
Telephone Nº: –

GROUND INFORMATION
Away Supporters' Entrances & Sections:
No usual segregation

ADMISSION INFO (2011/2012 PRICES)
Adult Standing: £8.00
Adult Seating: £8.00
Concessionary Standing: £5.00
Concessionary Seating: £5.00
Note: Under-16s are admitted free of charge when accompanying a paying adult
Programme Price: £1.00

DISABLED INFORMATION
Wheelchairs: Accommodated
Helpers: Admitted
Prices: Normal prices apply for the disabled and helpers
Disabled Toilets: None
Contact: (020) 8660-5491 – Becky Jones

Travelling Supporters' Information:
Routes: Exit the M25 at Junction 6 and head north on the A22 (signposted for London). Pass by Caterham and take the first exit at Whyteleafe Roundabout into Whyteleafe Hill then turn left into Church Road. The ground is on the left hand side of the road after a short distance.

WORTHING FC

Founded: 1886
Former Names: Worthing Association FC
Nickname: 'The Rebels'
Ground: Woodside Road, Worthing BN14 7HQ
Record Attendance: 3,600 (1936)
Pitch Size: 112 × 70 yards
Colours: Red shirts and shorts
Telephone Nº: (01903) 239575
Fax Number: (01903) 234795
Ground Capacity: 3,650
Seating Capacity: 500
Web site: www.worthingfc.com

GENERAL INFORMATION
Car Parking: Street parking only
Coach Parking: Street parking only
Nearest Railway Station: Worthing Central (½ mile)
Nearest Bus Station: Worthing
Club Shop: At the ground
Opening Times: Matchdays only
Telephone Nº: (01903) 239575

GROUND INFORMATION
Away Supporters' Entrances & Sections:
No usual segregation

ADMISSION INFO (2011/2012 PRICES)
Adult Standing: £9.00 **Adult Seating:** £9.50
Senior Citizen/Student Standing: £5.00
Senior Citizen/Student Seating: £5.50
Under-16s Standing: Free when accompanying a paying adult. £4.00 otherwise
Under-16s Seating: Admission charge if applicable + 50p
Programme Price: £2.00

DISABLED INFORMATION
Wheelchairs: Accommodated
Helpers: Admitted
Prices: Normal prices apply
Disabled Toilets: Available
Contact: (01903) 239575

Travelling Supporters' Information:
Routes: Take the A24/A27 to Worthing and at the Warren (or Grove Lodge) roundabout take the exit towards the Town Centre. Turn immediately right to keep Broadwater Green on your left and follow into South Farm Road. Go straight on at the next 5 mini-roundabouts then take the 3rd turning on the right into Pavilion Road. Turn right for Woodside Road.

Ryman League Premier Division 2010/2011 Season	AFC Hornchurch	Aveley	Billericay Town	Bury Town	Canvey Island	Carshalton Athletic	Concord Rangers	Cray Wanderers	Croydon Athletic	Folkestone Invicta	Harrow Borough	Hastings United	Hendon	Horsham	Kingstonian	Lowestoft Town	Maidstone United	Margate	Sutton United	Tonbridge Angels	Tooting & Mitcham United	Wealdstone
AFC Hornchurch		1-0	1-1	1-1	0-3	4-0	2-0	1-0	1-0	4-0	2-0	1-0	0-0	0-2	1-1	1-2	2-0	2-1	1-1	3-1	2-2	2-2
Aveley	1-4		0-1	0-2	1-3	2-0	1-1	0-3	3-0	1-1	0-2	1-3	0-2	1-0	1-1	0-3	1-2	1-1	0-0	0-3	3-1	0-1
Billericay Town	2-0	1-0		1-2	1-0	0-0	2-1	3-2	1-2	4-2	1-3	3-0	2-0	2-1	0-1	1-3	1-0	0-0	1-0	3-0	1-0	1-0
Bury Town	1-3	2-1	3-0		2-1	3-0	1-2	2-2	1-0	1-1	2-5	2-1	2-2	2-0	0-0	0-0	1-2	2-1	2-1	1-2	2-1	1-0
Canvey Island	3-0	2-1	3-2	3-0		1-1	0-4	4-2	3-2	1-0	2-0	2-2	4-1	3-1	0-2	0-0	3-0	2-0	1-3	1-0	0-2	1-1
Carshalton Athletic	0-0	2-2	1-3	1-0	1-0		2-4	1-1	1-2	1-0	0-1	1-1	2-1	0-0	1-3	2-0	0-0	1-3	0-2	3-2	2-0	2-3
Concord Rangers	1-3	0-1	1-1	2-2	1-0	1-1		2-0	3-0	2-1	3-0	2-1	3-2	2-0	2-1	0-2	3-2	0-0	0-0	1-2	3-0	1-6
Cray Wanderers	1-2	3-0	1-3	2-1	0-0	2-1	2-1		4-0	0-1	5-1	2-0	3-1	1-1	2-0	0-1	2-1	2-0	0-2	0-1	2-3	1-0
Croydon Athletic	0-3	0-2	0-0	1-3	0-4	1-4	1-3	3-1		2-1	1-3	2-0	1-4	2-4	0-4	0-2	1-2	5-3	0-3	2-0	0-1	2-2
Folkestone Invicta	1-1	1-2	1-1	0-2	1-2	1-2	1-1	1-1	0-2		1-0	1-3	1-2	0-0	1-0	1-4	4-0	1-2	0-2	0-0	1-3	1-1
Harrow Borough	1-0	1-2	1-1	2-0	6-1	2-1	0-2	1-1	3-1	2-0		2-2	2-3	6-0	1-0	2-0	2-0	0-0	0-0	2-0	2-0	2-4
Hastings United	0-1	2-3	1-0	0-2	0-1	0-1	0-3	1-1	3-1	2-2	2-0		1-1	2-3	1-2	0-0	1-2	3-0	2-3	1-2	3-2	2-0
Hendon	2-1	1-2	1-1	3-3	0-3	1-0	4-1	2-2	4-0	2-1	0-3	0-0		4-0	2-3	1-1	2-3	2-3	1-0	0-3	4-1	0-1
Horsham	0-0	0-0	1-2	1-4	1-1	2-1	1-3	0-4	1-1	0-0	1-7	1-1	1-2		2-3	1-2	1-1	1-1	3-1	0-2	1-0	2-1
Kingstonian	2-1	2-0	4-2	1-1	3-1	0-1	0-3	2-1	0-1	1-3	3-1	3-0	1-3		2-0	0-1	1-0	1-0	1-1	4-2	1-3	
Lowestoft Town	2-0	1-0	1-1	0-1	1-1	0-0	2-0	0-1	4-0	4-1	3-0	1-1	8-1	4-0	1-1		3-3	2-1	0-0	0-0	0-0	0-0
Maidstone United	0-0	1-1	0-2	1-2	0-1	1-3	2-0	2-4	0-1	2-0	0-0	2-4	2-2	0-1	1-2	0-1		0-2	0-1	0-3	1-1	2-4
Margate	2-2	2-0	0-1	0-1	2-2	2-1	1-2	0-2	0-2	2-3	2-0	1-1	6-1	3-3	0-3	1-1	3-2		0-1	3-3	1-0	
Sutton United	3-0	2-1	1-0	2-1	2-0	2-0	1-1	5-0	1-0	2-1	3-0	2-0	2-1	5-1	2-1		2-2	2-2		4-3		
Tonbridge Angels	7-1	1-0	3-1	2-3	1-1	4-0	3-2	0-4	1-0	1-0	1-2	2-0	2-1	2-0	1-1	3-3	1-0	1-1	0-1		3-3	2-0
Tooting & Mitcham United	1-1	1-2	3-2	1-3	1-2	0-5	3-2	0-3	2-2	4-1	3-2	1-1	4-3	2-2	1-1	2-1	3-4	3-0	0-3	1-5		1-0
Wealdstone	0-3	2-0	1-0	0-0	3-3	0-3	1-3	0-1	4-3	1-1	1-1	2-1	1-0	3-0	2-1	0-2	1-1	0-1	2-1	0-0	3-0	

Ryman League Division One North 2010/2011 Season	AFC Sudbury	Brentwood Town	Cheshunt	East Thurrock United	Enfield Town	Grays Athletic	Great Wakering Rovers	Harlow Town	Heybridge Swifts	Ilford	Maldon & Tiptree	Needham Market	Potters Bar Town	Redbridge	Romford	Thamesmead Town	Tilbury	Waltham Abbey	Waltham Forest	Ware	Wingate & Finchley
AFC Sudbury	■	2-1	2-2	0-2	1-5	3-3	4-0	1-0	2-1	1-1	6-3	2-2	6-0	3-0	0-4	2-1	0-0	2-4	3-3	5-1	1-1
Brentwood Town	2-3	■	1-1	1-3	0-6	2-1	4-0	1-1	3-3	2-1	1-2	2-4	1-0	2-0	2-0	3-0	2-0	2-2	3-1	2-1	2-3
Cheshunt	0-2	1-3	■	0-1	0-3	0-3	2-0	0-3	1-1	5-2	1-2	2-0	1-0	1-3	2-3	2-0	1-2	2-1	1-0	3-1	0-4
East Thurrock United	4-2	2-2	3-3	■	2-0	4-0	3-2	3-0	1-2	2-1	1-0	2-1	3-1	4-1	3-0	0-2	3-2	2-1	4-1	3-0	2-1
Enfield Town	2-0	0-1	1-2	0-4	■	2-0	0-3	5-0	3-0	1-0	0-1	0-0	2-3	2-1	1-1	0-1	2-0	2-1	3-0	4-0	1-2
Grays Athletic	1-1	0-0	9-0	1-3	2-0	■	1-2	0-1	1-1	3-0	1-1	2-3	1-2	2-2	3-0	4-1	3-1	1-0	4-0	1-1	2-1
Great Wakering Rovers	0-4	2-7	4-1	1-1	1-3	0-1	■	1-1	2-1	4-2	1-2	0-1	5-6	1-3	0-1	2-0	2-0	1-3	2-2	3-2	3-2
Harlow Town	1-0	0-4	3-4	1-1	2-2	1-2	1-0	■	2-1	2-0	3-0	1-2	3-0	1-1	4-1	2-1	1-0	1-2	3-1	1-1	1-0
Heybridge Swifts	5-1	0-3	5-2	1-3	2-2	3-1	1-2	1-2	■	7-2	4-0	0-1	2-0	2-3	2-3	4-0	1-0	1-1	1-1	2-1	2-2
Ilford	0-1	2-0	1-0	0-4	0-1	0-2	1-3	0-2	1-4	■	0-1	1-2	1-0	2-0	3-2	1-0	1-2	1-1	0-1	0-3	1-3
Maldon & Tiptree	1-1	1-1	3-1	0-1	2-4	1-2	3-1	4-1	2-4	1-1	■	2-2	2-2	3-2	2-0	1-1	2-1	2-1	4-1	3-2	0-0
Needham Market	3-2	0-0	3-2	3-0	3-2	1-1	3-2	1-1	0-0	3-3	4-0	■	1-0	7-1	2-1	3-1	2-1	4-2	4-0	3-2	4-1
Potters Bar Town	2-2	0-0	1-0	0-2	1-0	2-3	2-2	0-1	2-1	0-1	0-2	2-2	■	2-2	1-2	4-1	1-0	0-4	0-0	4-0	4-4
Redbridge	0-1	4-0	0-0	0-3	0-2	1-1	2-1	1-2	1-4	1-1	0-5	0-5	2-1	■	1-3	1-2	1-1	2-2	4-1	1-1	1-2
Romford	1-3	0-2	2-1	0-2	2-0	2-0	3-0	2-4	0-0	3-3	3-1	1-3	1-3	3-1	■	0-3	0-3	2-3	5-1	3-0	1-1
Thamesmead Town	2-2	1-2	1-1	1-2	0-3	0-2	0-1	1-2	2-1	2-2	3-3	0-2	0-3	0-2	1-1	■	3-1	3-0	1-0	3-1	0-3
Tilbury	1-2	0-2	0-0	0-2	0-4	3-2	3-1	2-0	3-4	2-0	0-2	3-2	1-2	0-2	3-3	0-1	■	2-1	1-0	0-2	1-2
Waltham Abbey	0-2	5-2	1-1	2-2	0-2	2-0	2-1	0-1	1-1	6-2	3-2	0-2	2-2	1-0	0-1	2-0	4-0	■	5-4	3-0	2-4
Waltham Forest	3-2	0-3	2-1	0-2	2-3	0-2	0-0	1-2	1-2	2-2	4-0	1-3	1-3	2-1	1-1	1-2	0-2	1-1	■	4-1	0-2
Ware	2-2	1-3	3-1	3-2	2-1	3-0	4-2	2-2	0-1	1-2	0-4	4-3	2-0	1-2	0-2	4-1	1-0	0-1	2-0	■	0-0
Wingate & Finchley	0-3	2-1	2-1	2-1	2-2	1-1	0-2	2-1	1-3	1-0	3-0	2-1	2-4	2-1	1-0	1-0	2-0	3-3	5-0	0-2	■

Ryman League Division One South 2010/2011 Season	Bognor Regis Town	Burgess Hill Town	Chatham Town	Chipstead	Corinthian-Casuals	Dulwich Hamlet	Eastbourne Town	Faversham Town	Fleet Town	Godalming Town	Horsham YMCA	Leatherhead	Merstham	Metropolitan Police	Ramsgate	Sittingbourne	Walton & Hersham	Walton Casuals	Whitehawk	Whitstable Town	Whyteleafe	Worthing
Bognor Regis Town		4-1	3-1	3-0	2-2	2-0	1-3	2-0	5-0	2-0	4-1	3-2	3-3	1-0	1-1	4-1	4-0	2-0	2-1	1-1	1-0	3-1
Burgess Hill Town	2-1		1-1	3-0	1-1	1-1	1-1	1-1	6-0	3-1	4-0	0-2	1-2	2-2	1-1	3-1	2-3	2-2	2-2	1-1	4-0	2-0
Chatham Town	1-1	1-0		0-3	1-0	3-2	3-1	0-2	4-1	0-2	0-1	1-1	4-4	2-3	0-2	1-2	3-2	3-2	1-6	0-0	1-2	1-1
Chipstead	1-3	2-1	2-2		3-1	1-4	1-1	2-1	2-4	2-1	2-1	1-3	2-2	2-2	1-1	0-1	0-0	2-1	1-1	2-2	1-2	2-0
Corinthian-Casuals	1-2	4-0	2-1	2-0		3-1	0-3	1-1	1-2	1-3	3-1	1-2	2-1	0-4	2-0	3-2	1-3	1-1	3-4	2-2	3-2	1-1
Dulwich Hamlet	1-2	1-2	5-2	3-2	3-1		2-2	2-2	6-0	4-0	1-1	1-0	0-1	0-1	2-4	3-0	2-0	1-2	0-1	2-0	1-0	1-2
Eastbourne Town	1-2	2-4	2-3	2-0	0-0	0-3		4-1	1-1	1-0	4-4	1-2	0-1	1-2	0-1	4-4	2-1	0-0	3-5	1-2	2-2	1-3
Faversham Town	4-0	1-1	2-1	2-2	3-0	1-2	3-0		2-2	3-1	2-0	0-0	0-0	0-2	0-2	3-1	2-0	0-1	2-1	1-1	1-0	2-2
Fleet Town	0-2	0-2	3-1	1-1	1-0	2-2	3-1	1-1		2-0	4-2	1-3	1-1	0-2	2-1	1-0	0-3	3-1	3-3	3-2	1-2	1-1
Godalming Town	0-6	1-1	2-0	0-0	2-1	3-5	0-1	0-0	0-5		3-0	1-2	2-0	1-2	0-2	1-3	4-3	0-3	1-2	4-1	2-2	
Horsham YMCA	0-3	1-4	1-1	2-2	0-3	0-2	3-2	0-1	2-0	0-2		0-11	3-5	3-0	2-3	0-5	0-2	0-3	2-2	2-3	2-1	1-1
Leatherhead	3-2	1-0	2-0	1-2	0-1	2-0	7-3	3-0	2-1	0-2	6-0		4-0	0-2	3-3	2-0	2-1	2-2	2-1	3-0	1-1	1-1
Merstham	2-4	0-1	0-2	0-4	3-1	2-3	1-1	1-1	5-2	1-0	2-2	0-3		0-3	1-2	1-1	2-2	1-5	1-4	4-3	0-3	3-3
Metropolitan Police	1-1	3-0	2-2	3-1	5-0	4-0	1-1	2-0	4-1	8-1	3-1	1-0	1-0		3-0	1-0	4-2	2-0	0-3	5-2	4-5	0-3
Ramsgate	1-3	1-3	2-1	0-1	3-1	0-0	3-1	2-2	2-2	1-0	2-2	0-2	0-1	1-1		0-2	1-1	5-1	2-2	0-1	5-0	3-3
Sittingbourne	0-5	0-1	2-0	0-3	1-0	2-2	0-1	1-1	2-1	2-2	1-0	1-2	1-1	0-2	3-0		0-3	1-0	2-2	2-0	2-1	0-4
Walton & Hersham	1-1	1-1	0-0	1-2	1-1	0-2	0-1	3-2	3-2	0-2	3-0	0-2	3-1	0-2	3-0	0-1		1-0	0-2	3-1	1-3	3-1
Walton Casuals	1-2	3-0	2-0	2-1	2-1	2-2	1-0	1-2	2-1	1-1	2-0	0-5	3-0	1-4	2-3	2-2	1-3		0-1	1-2	4-1	3-1
Whitehawk	1-2	6-0	4-1	3-1	6-0	3-1	3-0	2-2	2-0	5-0	6-1	2-1	1-1	0-2	4-2	4-0	0-1	1-0		1-1	5-0	1-0
Whitstable Town	1-1	1-1	2-1	0-3	0-0	0-1	1-2	0-1	2-3	1-2	4-0	2-2	1-0	0-6	1-0	2-1	1-1	2-2	1-3		3-4	3-2
Whyteleafe	1-5	2-3	0-1	1-2	4-2	2-1	2-3	1-0	3-4	2-1	2-0	2-6	1-1	1-2	0-1	0-1	2-5	4-0	1-2	3-2		1-2
Worthing	2-2	2-0	3-1	4-1	3-0	1-4	1-0	0-1	3-3	2-3	5-0	1-2	3-3	2-3	1-2	1-2	1-6	2-3	0-0	1-2	4-0	

Ryman Football League
Premier Division
Season 2010/2011

Sutton United	42	26	9	7	76	33	87
Tonbridge Angels	42	22	10	10	71	45	76
Bury Town	42	22	10	10	67	49	76
Lowestoft Town	42	20	15	7	68	30	75
Harrow Borough	42	22	7	13	77	51	73
Canvey Island	42	21	10	11	69	51	73
Kingstonian	42	21	9	12	66	50	72
Concord Rangers	42	21	8	13	72	55	71
Cray Wanderers	42	20	9	13	72	46	69
AFC Hornchurch	42	19	12	11	60	46	69
Billericay Town	42	20	9	13	56	45	69
Wealdstone	42	16	10	16	58	54	58
Carshalton Athletic	42	14	10	18	49	57	52
Tooting & Mitcham United	42	13	10	19	63	85	49
Hendon	42	12	10	20	61	81	46
Margate	42	11	12	19	52	64	45
Horsham	42	11	11	20	43	77	44
Hastings United	42	9	11	22	50	65	38
Aveley	42	10	8	24	35	62	38
Maidstone United	42	9	10	23	43	75	37
Croydon Athletic	42	10	4	28	44	95	31
Folkestone Invicta	42	5	12	25	34	68	27

Croydon Athletic had 3 points deducted.

Promotion Play-offs

Bury Town 1   Lowestoft Town 2
Tonbridge Angels 3   Harrow Borough .... 2 (aet.)

Tonbridge Angels 4   Lowestoft Town 3

Promoted: Sutton United and Tonbridge Angels

Relegated: Aveley, Maidstone United, Croydon Athletic and Folkestone Invicta

Ryman Football League
Division One North
Season 2010/2011

East Thurrock United	40	30	5	5	92	38	95
Needham Market	40	26	9	5	95	49	87
Wingate & Finchley	40	21	9	10	72	54	72
Harlow Town	40	21	8	11	61	51	71
Brentwood Town	40	20	9	11	75	55	69
Enfield Town	40	21	5	14	76	44	68
AFC Sudbury	40	18	12	10	82	64	66
Maldon & Tiptree	40	18	9	13	70	67	63
Heybridge Swifts	40	17	10	13	81	59	61
Grays Athletic	40	17	10	13	69	51	61
Waltham Abbey	40	16	10	14	75	63	58
Romford	40	16	7	17	63	66	55
Potters Bar Town	40	14	9	17	60	68	51
Ware	40	13	6	21	57	77	45
Great Wakering Rovers	40	13	5	22	60	82	44
Redbridge	40	10	9	21	51	79	39
Thamesmead Town	40	11	6	23	42	71	39
Cheshunt	40	10	8	22	49	81	38
Tilbury	40	11	4	25	41	66	37
Ilford	40	8	8	24	42	81	32
Waltham Forest	40	6	8	26	43	90	26

Leyton withdrew from Division One North on 14th January 2011 and were subsequently expelled from the League. The club's record at the time was expunged when it stood at:
19 1 6 12 13 45 9
Waltham Forest were reprieved from relegation due to this withdrawal.

Promotion Play-offs

Needham Market 1   Brentwood Town 3
Wingate & Finchley 4   Harlow Town 2

Wingate & Finchley 3   Brentwood Town .... 2 (aet)

Promoted: East Thurrock United and Wingate & Finchley

Ryman Football League
Division One South
Season 2010/2011

Metropolitan Police	42	30	6	6	102	41	96
Bognor Regis Town	42	29	9	4	103	43	96
Whitehawk	42	26	10	6	109	44	88
Leatherhead	42	27	7	8	100	41	88
Dulwich Hamlet	42	19	8	15	79	59	65
Walton & Hersham	42	18	8	16	69	58	62
Burgess Hill Town	42	16	14	12	69	60	62
Ramsgate	42	16	12	14	65	63	60
Faversham Town	42	14	17	11	55	48	59
Chipstead	42	15	12	15	63	67	57
Sittingbourne	42	16	8	18	52	66	56
Walton Casuals	42	15	8	19	65	71	53
Fleet Town	42	14	10	18	68	90	52
Worthing	42	12	14	16	76	72	50
Whitstable Town	42	12	13	17	58	75	49
Whyteleafe	42	14	3	25	65	94	45
Godalming Town	42	13	6	23	52	82	45
Eastbourne Town	42	11	11	20	60	78	44
Merstham	42	10	15	17	60	85	44
Corinthian-Casuals	42	11	9	22	53	80	42
Chatham Town	42	10	10	22	52	80	40
Horsham YMCA	42	5	8	29	41	119	23

Merstham had one point deducted.
Chatham Town were reprieved from relegation after transferring to the Isthmian League Division One North for the next season.

Promotion Play-offs

Bognor Regis Town 1   Dulwich Hamlet 3
Whitehawk 1   Leatherhead .... 1 (aet)
Leatherhead won 4-3 on penalties

Leatherhead 4   Dulwich Hamlet .... 3 (aet)

Promoted: Metropolitan Police and Leatherhead
Relegated: Horsham YMCA

F.A. Trophy 2010/2011

Qualifying 1	AFC Hornchurch	2	Brentwood Town	1
Qualifying 1	AFC Totton	5	AFC Hayes	0
Qualifying 1	Almondsbury Town	1	Didcot Town	0
Qualifying 1	Arlesey Town	0	Ramsgate	0
Qualifying 1	Ashford Town (Middlesex)	6	North Greenford United	2
Qualifying 1	Banbury United	1	Wimborne Town	1
Qualifying 1	Bideford	4	Tiverton Town	2
Qualifying 1	Biggleswade Town	0	Billericay Town	1
Qualifying 1	Bognor Regis Town	1	Croydon Athletic	0
Qualifying 1	Bridgwater Town	1	Stourbridge	3
Qualifying 1	Burnham	0	Brackley Town	0
Qualifying 1	Burscough	0	Clitheroe	2
Qualifying 1	Bury Town	2	Barton Rovers	0
Qualifying 1	Buxton	1	Stocksbridge Park Steels	2
Qualifying 1	Cambridge City	1	Aveley	0
Qualifying 1	Cammell Laird	1	Witton Albion	2
Qualifying 1	Canvey Island	1	AFC Sudbury	2
Qualifying 1	Carlton Town	1	Rushall Olympic	1
Qualifying 1	Carshalton Athletic	2	Ilford	0
Qualifying 1	Chesham United	1	Salisbury City	1
Qualifying 1	Chorley	1	Quorn	0
Qualifying 1	Cinderford Town	2	Hungerford Town	2
Qualifying 1	Cirencester Town	3	Halesowen Town	0
Qualifying 1	Colwyn Bay	2	Bradford Park Avenue	0
Qualifying 1	Cray Wanderers	2	Wingate & Finchley	1
Qualifying 1	Curzon Ashton	3	Skelmersdale United	1
Qualifying 1	Dulwich Hamlet	2	Hastings United	2
Qualifying 1	Durham City	0	FC Halifax Town	2
Qualifying 1	Enfield Town	2	Walton Casuals	1
Qualifying 1	Evesham United	1	Frome Town	0
Qualifying 1	FC United of Manchester	5	Newcastle Town	0
Qualifying 1	Faversham Town	1	Kingstonian	2
Qualifying 1	Fleet Town	0	Godalming Town	2
Qualifying 1	Folkestone Invicta	4	Worthing	2
Qualifying 1	Glapwell	2	Stamford	0
Qualifying 1	Great Wakering Rovers	1	Thamesmead Town	2
Qualifying 1	Harlow Town	3	Bedford Town	2
Qualifying 1	Harrogate Railway Athletic	2	Ossett Albion	1
Qualifying 1	Harrow Borough	0	Hendon	1
Qualifying 1	Hednesford Town	1	Whitby Town	2
Qualifying 1	Hemel Hempstead Town	2	Rugby Town	3
Qualifying 1	Horsham	3	Redbridge	0
Qualifying 1	Kendal Town	3	Frickley Athletic	0
Qualifying 1	Lancaster City	4	Ossett Town	2
Qualifying 1	Maidstone United	2	Burgess Hill Town	0
Qualifying 1	Margate	5	Whitehawk	1
Qualifying 1	Marine	2	Ashton United	2
Qualifying 1	Matlock Town	10	Bedworth United	0
Qualifying 1	Mickleover Sports	2	Hucknall Town	1

Round	Home	Score	Away	Score	
Qualifying 1	Market Drayton Town	1	Worksop Town	1	
Qualifying 1	North Ferriby United	0	Bamber Bridge	2	
Qualifying 1	Nantwich Town	6	Prescot Cables	2	
Qualifying 1	Needham Market	2	Lowestoft Town	2	
Qualifying 1	Northwich Victoria	0	Lincoln United	0	
Qualifying 1	Oxford City	1	Daventry Town	4	
Qualifying 1	Paulton Rovers	3	North Leigh	3	
Qualifying 1	Radcliffe Borough	1	Garforth Town	1	
Qualifying 1	Retford United	2	Romulus	2	
Qualifying 1	Sheffield	1	Chasetown	1	
Qualifying 1	Shepshed Dynamo	1	Mossley	4	
Qualifying 1	Slough Town	1	Chippenham Town	1	
Qualifying 1	Soham Town Rangers	1	Grays Athletic	2	
Qualifying 1	Sutton United	3	Tooting & Mitcham United	1	
Qualifying 1	Swindon Supermarine	4	Beaconsfield SYCOB	2	
Qualifying 1	Tonbridge Angels	3	Concord Rangers	2	
Qualifying 1	Truro City	1	Bishop's Cleeve	0	
Qualifying 1	Uxbridge	4	Abingdon United	1	
Qualifying 1	Waltham Forest	0	Romford	2	
Qualifying 1	Wealdstone	2	Potters Bar Town	2	
Qualifying 1	Weymouth	2	Bashley	1	
Qualifying 1	Windsor & Eton	1	Aylesbury	1	
Qualifying 1	Woodford United	1	Leamington	3	
Replay	Ashton United	1	Marine	3	
Replay	Aylesbury	1	Windsor & Eton	2	
Replay	Brackley Town	4	Burnham	0	
Replay	Chasetown	3	Sheffield	1	
Replay	Chippenham Town	4	Slough Town	1	
Replay	Garforth Town	1	Radcliffe Borough	2	
Replay	Hastings United	1	Dulwich Hamlet	2	
Replay	Hungerford Town	1	Cinderford Town	2	(aet)
Replay	Lincoln United	2	Northwich Victoria	3	
Replay	Lowestoft Town	6	Needham Market	2	
Replay	North Leigh	1	Paulton Rovers	2	
Replay	Potters Bar Town	1	Wealdstone	3	
Replay	Ramsgate	2	Arlesey Town	3	(aet)
Replay	Romulus	2	Retford United	1	
Replay	Rushall Olympic	4	Carlton Town	1	
Replay	Salisbury City	2	Chesham United	1	
Replay	Wimborne Town	1	Banbury United	3	(aet)
Replay	Worksop Town	1	Market Drayton Town	0	
Qualifying 2	AFC Sudbury	5	Hendon	1	
Qualifying 2	AFC Totton	1	Romford	3	
Qualifying 2	Arlesey Town	2	Uxbridge	2	
Qualifying 2	Ashford Town (Middlesex)	2	Bury Town	1	
Qualifying 2	Bideford	1	Dulwich Hamlet	0	
Qualifying 2	Billericay Town	2	Banbury United	1	
Qualifying 2	Bognor Regis Town	1	Godalming Town	1	
Qualifying 2	Brackley Town	4	Windsor & Eton	0	
Qualifying 2	Chippenham Town	1	Lowestoft Town	1	
Qualifying 2	Chorley	3	Marine	1	

Qualifying 2	Cirencester Town	2	Weymouth	1	
Qualifying 2	Cray Wanderers	1	Maidstone United	2	
Qualifying 2	Curzon Ashton	2	FC Halifax Town	1	
Qualifying 2	Daventry Town	1	Cambridge City	2	
Qualifying 2	Evesham United	0	Sutton United	1	
Qualifying 2	FC United of Manchester	2	Colwyn Bay	1	
Qualifying 2	Folkestone Invicta	0	Thamesmead Town	0	
Qualifying 2	Grays Athletic	2	Cinderford Town	1	
Qualifying 2	Harlow Town	2	Carshalton Athletic	0	
Qualifying 2	Kendal Town	1	Matlock Town	1	
Qualifying 2	Kingstonian	3	Wealdstone	5	
Qualifying 2	Leamington	3	Bamber Bridge	0	
Qualifying 2	Lowestoft Town	3	Chippenham Town	1	(aet)
Qualifying 2	Margate	1	AFC Hornchurch	2	
Qualifying 2	Mickleover Sports	2	Chasetown	5	
Qualifying 2	Mossley	2	Nantwich Town	3	
Qualifying 2	Northwich Victoria	4	Glapwell	0	
Qualifying 2	Paulton Rovers	4	Swindon Supermarine	5	
Qualifying 2	Radcliffe Borough	1	Witton Albion	1	
Qualifying 2	Romulus	1	Harrogate Railway Athletic	2	
Qualifying 2	Rushall Olympic	0	Stourbridge	1	
Qualifying 2	Salisbury City	2	Almondsbury Town	1	
Qualifying 2	Stocksbridge Park Steels	3	Rugby Town	2	
Qualifying 2	Tonbridge Angels	2	Enfield Town	0	
Qualifying 2	Truro City	2	Horsham	0	
Qualifying 2	Whitby Town	3	Clitheroe	1	
Qualifying 2	Worksop Town	2	Lancaster City	1	
Replay	Godalming Town	2	Bognor Regis Town	5	
Replay	Matlock Town	1	Kendal Town	2	
Replay	Thamesmead Town	1	Folkestone Invicta	3	
Replay	Uxbridge	4	Arlesey Town	2	
Replay	Witton Albion	3	Radcliffe Borough	1	
Qualifying 3	AFC Telford United	2	Corby Town	1	
Qualifying 3	Alfreton Town	4	Kendal Town	0	
Qualifying 3	Basingstoke Town	2	Havant & Waterlooville	2	
Qualifying 3	Bideford	0	AFC Hornchurch	3	
Qualifying 3	Blyth Spartans	1	Stafford Rangers	0	
Qualifying 3	Bognor Regis Town	2	Hampton & Richmond Borough	2	
Qualifying 3	Boreham Wood	3	Romford	0	
Qualifying 3	Boston United	2	Gainsborough Trinity	1	
Qualifying 3	Brackley Town	0	Wealdstone	1	
Qualifying 3	Braintree Town	2	Farnborough	0	
Qualifying 3	Bishop's Stortford	1	Ashford Town (Middlesex)	2	
Qualifying 3	Chorley	0	Guiseley	1	
Qualifying 3	Cirencester Town	2	Grays Athletic	3	
Qualifying 3	Curzon Ashton	2	Solihull Moors	1	
Qualifying 3	Dover Athletic	1	Woking	2	
Qualifying 3	Droylsden	3	Stourbridge	2	
Qualifying 3	Eastleigh	2	Folkestone Invicta	1	
Qualifying 3	Eastwood Town	2	Cambridge City	0	
Qualifying 3	Ebbsfleet United	4	Bromley	0	

Round	Team 1	Score	Team 2	Score
Qualifying 3	FC United of Manchester	1	Hinckley United	2
Qualifying 3	Harlow Town	3	Maidstone United	0
Qualifying 3	Harrogate Railway Athletic	3	Nantwich Town	4
Qualifying 3	Harrogate Town	1	Witton Albion	1
Qualifying 3	Leamington	1	Hyde	2
Qualifying 3	Lewes	1	Salisbury City	3
Qualifying 3	Lowestoft Town	2	Swindon Supermarine	1
Qualifying 3	Maidenhead United	2	Uxbridge	4
Qualifying 3	Nuneaton Town	1	Worcester City	2
Qualifying 3	Redditch United	80	Bye	0
Qualifying 3	St. Albans City	3	Staines Town	1
Qualifying 3	Sutton United	4	Billericay Town	2
Qualifying 3	Thurrock	0	Dartford	2
Qualifying 3	Truro City	1	AFC Sudbury	2
Qualifying 3	Vauxhall Motors (Cheshire)	1	Stalybridge Celtic	3
Qualifying 3	Welling United	1	Tonbridge Angels	0
Qualifying 3	Weston-Super-Mare	1	Dorchester Town	3
Qualifying 3	Whitby Town	2	Northwich Victoria	2
Qualifying 3	Workington	0	Chasetown	0
Qualifying 3	Worksop Town	1	Chelmsford City	0
Qualifying 3	Worksop Town	4	Stocksbridge Park Steels	1
Replay	Chasetown	4	Workington	0
Replay	Grays Athletic	0	Cirencester Town	1
Replay	Hampton & Richmond Borough	2	Bognor Regis Town	0
Replay	Havant & Waterlooville	1	Basingstoke Town	2
Replay	Northwich Victoria	1	Whitby Town	0
Replay	Witton Albion	1	Harrogate Town	2
Round 1	AFC Sudbury	1	Hampton & Richmond Borough	4
Round 1	AFC Wimbledon	3	Braintree Town	0
Round 1	Alfreton Town	3	Hyde	0
Round 1	Ashford Town (Middlesex)	1	AFC Hornchurch	0
Round 1	Barrow	2	Guiseley	3
Round 1	Basingstoke Town	0	Salisbury City	2
Round 1	Blyth Spartans	2	Fleetwood Town	0
Round 1	Cambridge United	2	Forest Green Rovers	1
Round 1	Chasetown	3	Kettering Town	3
Round 1	Cirencester Town	1	Gloucester City	1
Round 1	Crawley Town	3	Dartford	3
Round 1	Curzon Ashton	2	Altrincham	1
	The match was abandoned at half-time due to power failure and a replay was ordered.			
Round 1	Darlington	3	Tamworth	2
Round 1	Dorchester Town	3	St. Albans City	0
Round 1	Droylsden	4	Hinckley United	3
Round 1	Eastbourne Borough	3	Boreham Wood	1
Round 1	Eastleigh	1	Sutton United	1
Round 1	Ebbsfleet United	3	Hayes & Yeading United	1
Round 1	Gateshead	2	Southport	1
Round 1	Grimsby Town	3	Redditch United	0
Round 1	Harlow Town	0	Woking	2
Round 1	Harrogate Town	0	AFC Telford United	3
Round 1	Histon	2	Bath City	3

Round 1	Lowestoft Town	2	Uxbridge	3	
Round 1	Luton Town	0	Welling United	0	
Round 1	Newport County	0	Wealdstone	0	
Round 1	Rushden & Diamonds	1	Eastwood Town	1	
Round 1	Stalybridge Celtic	2	Nantwich Town	1	
Round 1	Worcester City	1	Northwich Victoria	0	
Round 1	Worksop Town	0	Mansfield Town	5	
	Match played at Retford				
Round 1	Wrexham	2	Kidderminster Harriers	0	
Round 1	York City	0	Boston United	1	
Replay	Curzon Ashton	0	Altrincham	2	
Replay	Dartford	1	Crawley Town	0	
Replay	Eastwood Town	4	Rushden & Diamonds	3	(aet)
Replay	Gloucester City	3	Cirencester Town	0	
Replay	Kettering Town	1	Chasetown	2	(aet)
Replay	Southport	0	Gateshead	1	
Replay	Sutton United	0	Eastleigh	4	
Replay	Wealdstone	0	Newport County	1	(aet)
Replay	Welling United	1	Luton Town	2	
Round 2	AFC Telford United	1	Eastwood Town	0	
Round 2	AFC Wimbledon	2	Woking	3	
Round 2	Alfreton Town	3	Cambridge United	3	
Round 2	Ashford Town (Middlesex)	0	Dartford	1	
Round 2	Blyth Spartans	2	Altrincham	1	
Round 2	Boston United	0	Gloucester City	1	
Round 2	Chasetown	2	Grimsby Town	1	
Round 2	Darlington	4	Bath City	1	
Round 2	Dorchester Town	3	Eastbourne Borough	3	
Round 2	Droylsden	1	Ebbsfleet United	0	
Round 2	Eastleigh	3	Worcester City	3	
Round 2	Gateshead	6	Hampton & Richmond Borough	0	
Round 2	Guiseley	2	Stalybridge Celtic	1	
Round 2	Luton Town	4	Uxbridge	0	
Round 2	Mansfield Town	4	Newport County	2	
Round 2	Salisbury City	1	Wrexham	0	
Replay	Cambridge United	3	Alfreton Town	6	(aet)
Replay	Eastbourne Borough	1	Dorchester Town	0	
Replay	Worcester City	1	Eastleigh	4	
Round 3	AFC Telford United	0	Darlington	3	
Round 3	Blyth Spartans	2	Droylsden	2	
Round 3	Eastbourne Borough	1	Guiseley	1	
Round 3	Eastleigh	1	Chasetown	3	
Round 3	Gateshead	3	Dartford	0	
Round 3	Luton Town	1	Gloucester City	0	
Round 3	Mansfield Town	1	Alfreton Town	1	
Round 3	Woking	0	Salisbury City	2	
Replay	Alfreton Town	1	Mansfield Town	2	
Replay	Droylsden	0	Blyth Spartans	4	
Replay	Guiseley	2	Eastbourne Borough	1	

Round 4	Blyth Spartans	0	Gateshead	2	
Round 4	Chasetown	2	Mansfield Town	2	
Round 4	Darlington	2	Salisbury City	1	
Round 4	Guiseley	0	Luton Town	1	
Replay	Mansfield Town	3	Chasetown	1	
Semi-finals					
1st leg	Darlington	3	Gateshead	2	
2nd leg	Gateshead	0	Darlington	0	
	Darlington won 3-2 on aggregate.				
1st leg	Mansfield Town	1	Luton Town	0	
2nd leg	Luton Town	1	Mansfield Town	1	(aet)
	Mansfield Town won 2-1 on aggregate				
FINAL	Darlington	1	Mansfield Town	0	

Cup Statistics provided by:

www.soccerdata.com

F.A. Vase 2010/2011

Round 1	AFC Dunstable	3	Colney Heath	1	
Round 1	AFC Emley	3	Runcorn Linnets	1	
Round 1	AFC Liverpool	3	Hallam	0	
Round 1	Atherton Laburnum Rovers	2	Runcorn Town	3	
Round 1	Aylesbury United	4	Hertford Town	3	(aet)
Round 1	Baldock Town Letchworth	0	Holyport	1	
Round 1	Barking	1	Flackwell Heath	2	
Round 1	Bedlington Terriers	0	Spennymoor Town	1	
Round 1	Bemerton Heath Harlequins	5	Lydney Town	2	(aet)
Round 1	Billingham Town	3	Ashington	4	(aet)
Round 1	Binfield	3	Hillingdon Borough	2	
Round 1	Bishop Auckland	3	Billingham Synthonia	4	(aet)
Round 1	Bishop Sutton	2	Keynsham Town	2	(aet)
Round 1	Blaby & Whetstone Athletic	2	Westfields	5	
Round 1	Bloxwich United	5	Pilkington XXX	0	
Round 1	Boldmere St. Michaels	1	Continental Star	0	
Round 1	Bookham	0	Herne Bay	4	
Round 1	Bracknell Town	2	Wodson Park	0	
Round 1	Brading Town	4	St. Francis Rangers	2	
Round 1	Brighouse Town	3	Eccleshill United	3	(aet)
Round 1	Brislington	0	St. Blazey	1	
Round 1	Burnham Ramblers	2	Kentish Town	0	(aet)
Round 1	Cadbury Heath	2	Wootton Bassett Town	1	
Round 1	Calne Town	1	Downton	2	
Round 1	Camberley Town	2	Blackfield & Langley	1	
Round 1	Cambridge Regional College	4	Wellingborough Town	0	
Round 1	Chalfont St. Peter	6	Newbury (2)	0	
Round 1	Clanfield 85	2	Fairford Town	1	
Round 1	Coalville Town	2	Stratford Town	1	
Round 1	Cockfosters	0	Witham Town	3	
Round 1	Colliers Wood United	5	Cove	2	
Round 1	Corinthian	0	Tunbridge Wells	4	
Round 1	Coventry Copsewood	2	Heath Town Rangers	1	
Round 1	Coventry Sphinx	4	Anstey Nomads	3	
Round 1	Crawley Down	0	Rye United	1	
Round 1	Croydon	3	Beckenham Town	7	
Round 1	Dunkirk	2	Blidworth Welfare	0	
Round 1	Dunstable Town	5	AFC Wallingford	0	
Round 1	Dunston UTS	2	Washington	1	
Round 1	Eccleshall	2	Bridgnorth Town	4	
Round 1	Egham Town	2	Molesey	0	
Round 1	Erith & Belvedere	2	Chichester City	1	(aet)
Round 1	Eton Manor	4	FC Clacton	2	
Round 1	Fisher	1	Warlingham	3	
Round 1	Forest Town	3	Greenwood Meadows	1	
Round 1	Formby	2	Flixton	0	
Round 1	Gedling Town	2	Glossop North End	1	
Round 1	Godmanchester Rovers	4	Framlingham Town	0	
Round 1	Gorleston	1	Hadleigh United	0	

Round	Home	Score	Away	Score	
Round 1	Guildford City (2)	3	Horley Town	2	(aet)
Round 1	Haringey Borough	1	Tring Athletic	3	
Round 1	Heanor Town	6	Clipstone Welfare	2	
Round 1	Holbrook Sports	4	Arnold Town	4	(aet)
Round 1	Holwell Sports	4	Tividale	3	
Round 1	Ilfracombe Town	1	Hengrove Athletic	2	
Round 1	Ipswich Wanderers	1	Walsham Le Willows	2	
Round 1	Irlam	2	Colne	0	
Round 1	Kidlington	0	Bitton	1	
Round 1	Lancing	1	Christchurch	1	(aet)
Round 1	Langford	1	Hullbridge Sports	3	
Round 1	Leeds Carnegie	4	Easington Colliery	0	
Round 1	Leiston	3	Haverhill Rovers	2	(aet)
Round 1	Leverstock Green	5	Enfield 1893	4	
Round 1	Lordswood	1	Three Bridges	2	
Round 1	Louth Town	3	Barton Town Old Boys	3	
Round 1	Lymington Town	1	Bournemouth (Ams)	2	
Round 1	Maine Road	2	AFC Blackpool	2	(aet)
Round 1	Malvern Town	2	Heather St. Johns	6	
Round 1	Melksham Town	3	Laverstock & Ford	1	
Round 1	Moneyfields	1	Greenwich Borough	0	
Round 1	Newport (IOW)	3	Shoreham	0	
Round 1	Northallerton Town	3	Stokesley	4	
Round 1	Odd Down	7	Bridport	0	
Round 1	Peacehaven & Telscombe	1	Hamble ASSC	0	
Round 1	Ramsbottom United	0	Staveley Miners Welfare	1	
Round 1	Raynes Park Vale	0	Hythe Town	3	
Round 1	Reading Town	4	Newport Pagnell Town	2	
Round 1	Rossendale United	0	Bacup Borough	2	
Round 1	Saltash United	9	Newquay	1	
Round 1	Scarborough Athletic	2	Bridlington Town	2	(aet)
Round 1	Sherborne Town	2	Bodmin Town	2	(aet)
Round 1	South Shields	0	Thackley	2	
Round 1	St. Helens Town	2	Oldham Boro	1	
	Match played at Ashton Town FC				
Round 1	St. Neots Town	11	Felixstowe & Walton United	0	
Round 1	Stansted	2	Takeley	0	
Round 1	Stanway Rovers	4	London APSA	0	
Round 1	Stone Dominoes	1	Heath Hayes	4	
Round 1	Tadcaster Albion	2	Tow Law Town	0	
Round 1	Thrapston Town	2	King's Lynn Town	4	
Round 1	Thurnby Nirvana	1	Shifnal Town	2	
Round 1	Torpoint Athletic	4	Radstock Town	1	
Round 1	Verwood Town	1	Budleigh Salterton	0	(aet)
Round 1	Wantage Town	2	Shrivenham	1	
Round 1	Wednesfield	4	Studley	3	
Round 1	Wellington	5	Tavistock	0	
Round 1	West Auckland Town	6	Birtley Town	0	
Round 1	Whitton United	2	Norwich United	0	
Round 1	Wick	0	VCD Athletic	2	(aet)
Round 1	Willenhall Town	0	Gornal Athletic	2	
Round 1	Winterton Rangers	3	Deeping Rangers	1	

Round	Home	Score	Away	Score	
Round 1	Wisbech Town	5	Cogenhoe United	1	
Round 1	Wolverhampton Casuals	1	Bustleholme	3	
Replay	AFC Blackpool	2	Maine Road	1	
Replay	Arnold Town	1	Holbrook Sports	3	
Replay	Barton Town Old Boys	1	Louth Town	0	(aet)
Replay	Bodmin Town	1	Sherborne Town	0	
Replay	Bridlington Town	1	Scarborough Athletic	3	
Replay	Christchurch	0	Lancing	1	
Replay	Eccleshill United	2	Brighouse Town	1	
Replay	Keynsham Town	1	Bishop Sutton	0	
Round 2	AFC Blackpool	0	AFC Liverpool	2	
Round 2	AFC Dunstable	1	Tring Athletic	2	
Round 2	Beckenham Town	2	Peacehaven & Telscombe	1	(aet)
Round 2	Billingham Synthonia	3	Stokesley	1	
Round 2	Bitton	2	Shortwood United	1	
Round 2	Boldmere St. Michaels	1	Gornal Athletic	2	
Round 2	Bootle	1	Shildon	3	
Round 2	Bournemouth (Ams)	5	Odd Down	0	
Round 2	Bridgnorth Town	2	Coalville Town	4	
Round 2	Bristol Manor Farm	3	Torpoint Athletic	7	
Round 2	Bustleholme	2	Barton Town Old Boys	0	
Round 2	Causeway United	2	Gedling Town	0	
Round 2	Chertsey Town	1	Moneyfields	2	
Round 2	Clanfield 85	0	Bemerton Heath Harlequins	3	
Round 2	Colliers Wood United	1	Witney United	0	
	Played at Croydon FC				
Round 2	Coventry Sphinx	0	Dunkirk	3	
Round 2	Dawlish Town	0	Bodmin Town	2	
Round 2	Downton	2	Cadbury Heath	3	
Round 2	Dunstable Town	2	Cambridge Regional College	1	
Round 2	Dunston UTS	4	AFC Emley	0	
Round 2	Eccleshill United	0	Runcorn Town	2	
Round 2	Egham Town	1	Newport (IOW)	2	
Round 2	Epsom & Ewell	4	Bracknell Town	0	
Round 2	Erith & Belvedere	0	Lancing	2	
Round 2	Flackwell Heath	1	Three Bridges	2	
Round 2	Forest Town	0	Tadcaster Albion	4	
Round 2	Formby	1	Bacup Borough	0	
Round 2	Godmanchester Rovers	0	Stanway Rovers	1	
Round 2	Gresley	2	Heanor Town	0	
Round 2	Guildford City	5	Brading Town	2	
Round 2	Heath Hayes	2	Tipton Town	1	
Round 2	Herne Bay	3	Camberley Town	0	
Round 2	Holbrook Sports	7	Holwell Sports	0	
Round 2	Hullbridge Sports	1	Leverstock Green	5	
Round 2	King's Lynn Town	4	Gorleston	0	
Round 2	Kirkley & Pakefield	0	Long Buckby	1	
Round 2	Leeds Carnegie	4	Marske United	3	(aet)
Round 2	New Mills	2	Ashington	4	
Round 2	Norton & Stockton Ancients	4	Irlam	3	
Round 2	Plymouth Parkway	6	Melksham Town	1	

Round 2	Poole Town	4	Wellington	3	
Round 2	Reading Town	1	Warlingham	0	
Round 2	Royston Town	2	Leiston	2	(aet)
Round 2	Rye United	4	Chalfont St. Peter	4	(aet)
	Match played at Sussex County Ground, Lancing				
Round 2	Scarborough Athletic	2	Armthorpe Welfare	2	(aet)
Round 2	Shifnal Town	2	Bloxwich United	2	(aet)
Round 2	St. Blazey	1	Hengrove Athletic	1	(aet)
Round 2	St. Ives Town	2	Aylesbury United	1	
Round 2	St. Neots Town	6	Burnham Ramblers	1	
Round 2	Stansted	3	Eton Manor	1	
Round 2	Staveley Miners Welfare	1	Pickering Town	0	(aet)
Round 2	Stotfold	2	Whitton United	1	
Round 2	Thackley	0	Whitley Bay	1	
Round 2	Tunbridge Wells	8	Holyport	0	
Round 2	VCD Athletic	1	Hythe Town	5	
Round 2	Verwood Town	2	Keynsham Town	1	
Round 2	Wantage Town	3	Binfield	1	
Round 2	Wednesfield	1	Heather St. Johns	3	(aet)
Round 2	West Auckland Town	1	Spennymoor Town	3	
Round 2	Westfields	3	Coventry Copsewood	0	
Round 2	Willand Rovers	2	Saltash United	1	
Round 2	Winterton Rangers	0	St. Helens Town	2	
Round 2	Witham Town	3	Walsham Le Willows	1	
Round 2	Wroxham	4	Wisbech Town	0	
Replay	Armthorpe Welfare	2	Scarborough Athletic	3	
Replay	Bloxwich United	5	Shifnal Town	3	
Replay	Chalfont St. Peter	1	Rye United	2	
Replay	Hengrove Athletic	0	St. Blazey	2	
Replay	Leiston	1	Royston Town	0	
Round 3	Beckenham Town	1	King's Lynn Town	2	
Round 3	Bitton	4	Newport (IOW)	1	
Round 3	Cadbury Heath	4	Reading Town	1	
Round 3	Causeway United	0	Norton & Stockton Ancients	3	
Round 3	Dunkirk	1	Ashington	2	
Round 3	Dunston UTS	2	Heather St. Johns	0	
Round 3	Epsom & Ewell	1	St. Neots Town	2	
Round 3	Formby	2	Tadcaster Albion	3	
Round 3	Gornal Athletic	0	Runcorn Town	3	
Round 3	Gresley	4	Bustleholme	2	
Round 3	Guildford City	4	Moneyfields	3	
Round 3	Heath Hayes	1	Bloxwich United	3	
Round 3	Herne Bay	2	Colliers Wood United	0	
Round 3	Holbrook Sports	4	St. Helens Town	0	
Round 3	Lancing	4	Witham Town	2	(aet)
Round 3	Leeds Carnegie	1	Staveley Miners Welfare	4	
Round 3	Leiston	3	Hythe Town	1	
Round 3	Leverstock Green	3	Tunbridge Wells	1	
Round 3	Plymouth Parkway	1	Bodmin Town	3	(aet)
Round 3	Poole Town	3	Wantage Town	2	
Round 3	Scarborough Athletic	0	Spennymoor Town	3	

Round 3	Shildon	0	Coalville Town	2	
Round 3	St. Blazey	1	Bemerton Heath Harlequins	2	
Round 3	Stanway Rovers	0	Stansted	1	
Round 3	Stotfold	0	Long Buckby	3	
Round 3	Three Bridges	1	Rye United	3	(aet)
Round 3	Tring Athletic	1	Dunstable Town	6	
Round 3	Verwood Town	2	Torpoint Athletic	5	
Round 3	Westfields	1	Billingham Synthonia	2	(aet)
Round 3	Whitley Bay	7	AFC Liverpool	1	
Round 3	Willand Rovers	2	Bournemouth (Ams)	1	
Round 3	Wroxham	0	St. Ives Town	1	(aet)
Round 4	Billingham Synthonia	2	Tadcaster Albion	1	
Round 4	Bitton	2	Coalville Town	3	
Round 4	Bloxwich United	2	Torpoint Athletic	3	
Round 4	Bodmin Town	1	Stansted	4	
Round 4	Cadbury Heath	1	Spennymoor Town	5	
Round 4	Dunstable Town	2	Willand Rovers	0	
Round 4	Gresley	1	St. Neots Town	3	
Round 4	Guildford City	2	Leiston	6	(aet)
Round 4	Herne Bay	1	Whitley Bay	2	
Round 4	Holbrook Sports	2	Lancing	1	
Round 4	Leverstock Green	4	Bemerton Heath Harlequins	1	
Round 4	Long Buckby	3	Ashington	2	
Round 4	Norton & Stockton Ancients	0	King's Lynn Town	1	
Round 4	Poole Town	3	St. Ives Town	2	
Round 4	Runcorn Town	1	Dunston UTS	3	
Round 4	Staveley Miners Welfare	0	Rye United	3	
Round 5	Coalville Town	3	Holbrook Sports	1	(aet)
Round 5	King's Lynn Town	2	St. Neots Town	1	
Round 5	Leiston	2	Long Buckby	1	
Round 5	Leverstock Green	1	Rye United	2	
Round 5	Poole Town	3	Spennymoor Town	2	
Round 5	Stansted	0	Dunston UTS	2	
Round 5	Torpoint Athletic	1	Billingham Synthonia	0	
Round 5	Whitley Bay	5	Dunstable Town	1	
Round 6	Coalville Town	1	Leiston	0	
Round 6	Dunston UTS	1	Whitley Bay	2	
Round 6	King's Lynn Town	3	Rye United	1	(aet)
Round 6	Poole Town	2	Torpoint Athletic	1	
Semi-finals					
1st leg	Coalville Town	3	King's Lynn Town	0	
2nd leg	King's Lynn Town	2	Coalville Town	3	
	Coalville Town won 6-2 on aggregate				
1st leg	Poole Town	1	Whitley Bay	2	
2nd leg	Whitley Bay	3	Poole Town	1	
	Whitley Bay won 5-2 on aggregate				
FINAL	Whitley Bay	3	Coalville Town	2	

ENGLAND INTERNATIONAL LINE-UPS AND STATISTICS 2010

18th June 2010
v ALGERIA (WCF)   *Cape Town*
D. James   Portsmouth
G. Johnson   Liverpool
A. Cole   Chelsea
S. Gerrard   Liverpool
J. Carragher   Liverpool
J. Terry   Chelsea
A. Lennon   Tottenham H. (sub. S. Wright-Phillips 63)
F. Lampard   Chelsea
E. Heskey   Aston Villa (sub. J. Defoe 74)
W. Rooney   Manchester United
G. Barry   Manchester City (sub. P. Crouch 84)
Result 0-0

23rd June 2010
v SLOVAKIA (WCF)   *Port Elizabeth*
D. James   Portsmouth
G. Johnson   Liverpool
A. Cole   Chelsea
S. Gerrard   Liverpool
M. Upson   West Ham United
J. Terry   Chelsea
J. Milner   Aston Villa
F. Lampard   Chelsea
J. Defoe   Tottenham H. (sub. E. Heskey 86)
W. Rooney   Manchester United (sub. J. Cole 72)
G. Barry   Manchester City
Result 1-0   Defoe

27th June 2010
v GERMANY (WCF)   *Bloemfontein*
D. James   Portsmouth
G. Johnson   Liverpool (sub. S. Wright-Phillips 87)
A. Cole   Chelsea
S. Gerrard   Liverpool
M. Upson   West Ham United
J. Terry   Chelsea
J. Milner   Aston Villa (sub. J. Cole 63)
F. Lampard   Chelsea
J. Defoe   Tottenham H. (sub. E. Heskey 71)
W. Rooney   Manchester United
G. Barry   Manchester City
Result 1-4   Upson

11th August 2010
v HUNGARY   *Wembley*
J. Hart   Manchester City
G. Johnson   Liverpool
A. Cole   Chelsea (sub. K. Gibbs 46)
S. Gerrard   Liverpool (sub. J. Wilshire 82)
P. Jagielka   Everton
J. Terry   Chelsea (sub. M. Dawson 46)
T. Walcott   Arsenal (sub. B. Zamora 46)
F. Lampard   Chelsea (sub. A. Young 46)
A. Johnson   Manchester City
W. Rooney   Manchester Utd. (sub. J. Milner 66)
G. Barry   Manchester City
Result 2-1   Gerrard 2

3rd September 2010
v BULGARIA (ECQ)   *Wembley*
J. Hart   Manchester City
G. Johnson   Liverpool
A. Cole   Chelsea
S. Gerrard   Liverpool
M. Dawson   Tottenham Hotspur (sub. G. Cahill 57)
P. Jagielka   Everton
T. Walcott   Arsenal (sub. A. Johnson 74)
G. Barry   Manchester City
J. Defoe   Tottenham Hotspur (sub. A. Young 87)
W. Rooney   Manchester United
J. Milner   Manchester City
Result 4-0   Defoe 3, Johnson

7th September 2010
v SWITZERLAND (ECQ)   *Basle*
J. Hart   Manchester City
G. Johnson   Liverpool
A. Cole   Chelsea
S. Gerrard   Liverpool
J. Lescott   Manchester City
P. Jagielka   Everton
T. Walcott   Arsenal (sub. A. Johnson 13)
G. Barry   Manchester City
J. Defoe   Tottenham Hotspur (sub. D. Bent 70)
W. Rooney   Man. Utd. (sub. S. Wright-Phillips 79)
J. Milner   Manchester City
Result 3-1   Rooney, Johnson, Bent

ENGLAND INTERNATIONAL LINE-UPS AND STATISTICS 2010-2011

12th October 2010
v MONTENEGRO (ECQ)   *Wembley*
J. Hart	Manchester City
G. Johnson	Liverpool
A. Cole	Chelsea
S. Gerrard	Liverpool
R. Ferdinand	Manchester United
J. Lescott	Manchester City
A. Young	Aston Villa (sub. S. Wright-Phillips 74)
G. Barry	Manchester City
P. Crouch	Tottenham Hotspur (sub. K. Davies 69)
W. Rooney	Manchester United
A. Johnson	Manchester City

Result 0-0

17th November 2010
v FRANCE   *Wembley*
B. Foster	Birmingham City
P. Jagielka	Everton
K. Gibbs	Arsenal (sub. S. Warnock 72)
S. Gerrard	Liverpool (sub. P. Crouch 84)
R. Ferdinand	Man. United (sub. M. Richards 46)
J. Lescott	Manchester City
T. Walcott	Arsenal (sub. A. Johnson 46)
J. Henderson	Sunderland
A. Caroll	Newcastle Utd. (sub. J. Bothroyd 72)
G. Barry	Manchester City (sub. A. Young 46)
J. Milner	Manchester City

Result 1-2   Crouch

9th February 2011
v DENMARK   *Copenhagen*
J. Hart	Manchester City
G. Johnson	Liverpool
A. Cole	Chelsea (sub. L. Baines 81)
J. Wilshere	Arsenal (sub. G. Barry 46)
M. Dawson	Tottenham Hotspur (sub. G. Cahill 60)
J. Terry	Chelsea
T. Walcott	Arsenal (sub. S. Downing 67)
F. Lampard	Chelsea (sub. S. Parker 46)
D. Bent	Aston Villa
W. Rooney	Manchester Utd. (sub. A. Young 46)
J. Milner	Manchester City

Result 2-1   Bent, Young

26th March 2011
v WALES (ECQ)   *Cardiff*
J. Hart	Manchester City
G. Johnson	Liverpool
A. Cole	Chelsea
S. Parker	West Ham Utd. (sub. P. Jagielka 88)
M. Dawson	Tottenham Hotspur
J. Terry	Chelsea
F. Lampard	Chelsea
J. Wilshere	Arsenal (sub. S. Downing 82)
D. Bent	Aston Villa
W. Rooney	Manchester Utd. (sub. J. Milner 70)
A. Young	Aston Villa

Result 2-0   Lampard (pen), Bent

29th March 2011
v GHANA   *Wembley*
J. Hart	Manchester City
G. Johnson	Liverpool (sub. J. Lescott 46)
L. Baines	Everton
G. Barry	Manchester City
G. Cahill	Bolton Wanderers
P. Jagielka	Everton
J. Milner	Manchester City
J. Wilshere	Arsenal (sub. M. Jarvis 69)
A. Caroll	Liverpool (sub. J. Defoe 59)
A. Young	Aston Villa (sub. D. Welbeck 81)
S. Downing	Aston Villa

Result 1-1   Carroll

4th June 2011
v SWITZERLAND (ECQ)   *Wembley*
J. Hart	Manchester City
G. Johnson	Liverpool
A. Cole	Chelsea (sub. L Baines 30)
S. Parker	West Ham United
R. Ferdinand	Manchester United
J. Terry	Chelsea
T. Walcott	Arsenal (sub. S. Downing 77)
F. Lampard	Chelsea (sub. A. Young 46)
D. Bent	Aston Villa
J. Wilshere	Arsenal
J. Milner	Manchester City

Result 2-2   Lampard (pen), Young

Ryman Football League Premier Division 2011/2012 Fixtures

	AFC Hornchurch	Aveley	Billericay Town	Bury Town	Canvey Island	Carshalton Athletic	Concord Rangers	Cray Wanderers	East Thurrock	Harrow Borough	Hastings United	Hendon	Horsham	Kingstonian	Leatherhead	Lewes	Lowestoft Town	Margate	Metropolitan Police	Tooting & Mitcham United	Wealdstone	Wingate & Finchley
AFC Hornchurch		17/12	09/04	04/10	23/08	26/11	03/03	17/03	28/01	10/12	04/02	05/11	27/08	15/10	28/04	18/02	02/01	14/01	31/03	10/09	24/09	01/10
Aveley	12/09		11/02	14/04	14/01	10/12	29/08	10/03	26/12	24/03	01/10	28/04	19/11	20/08	03/09	07/04	12/11	31/12	03/10	28/01	29/10	25/02
Billericay Town	26/12	26/11		29/08	29/10	07/04	13/09	25/02	14/04	31/12	04/10	04/02	10/03	03/09	20/08	24/03	28/04	10/12	28/01	01/10	12/11	14/01
Bury Town	21/01	24/09	02/01		17/12	07/01	27/09	21/04	19/11	18/02	27/08	23/08	17/03	05/11	08/10	03/03	09/04	15/10	10/09	03/12	31/03	11/02
Canvey Island	31/12	27/09	18/02	13/09		20/08	26/12	07/01	29/08	03/09	05/11	03/03	10/12	24/03	14/04	08/10	21/01	28/04	26/11	15/10	04/02	07/04
Carshalton Athletic	11/02	21/04	10/09	01/10	17/03		18/02	02/01	04/10	15/10	31/03	05/11	27/08	17/12	03/03	19/11	05/11	24/09	28/01	14/01	09/04	23/08	03/12
Concord Rangers	12/11	02/01	17/12	14/01	09/04	29/10		23/08	11/02	19/11	10/09	17/03	28/01	04/10	25/02	21/04	31/03	01/10	24/09	27/08	03/12	10/03
Cray Wanderers	21/08	05/11	15/10	10/12	01/10	29/08	31/12		03/09	07/04	03/03	26/11	28/04	28/01	25/03	14/04	05/02	27/12	18/02	14/01	04/10	13/09
East Thurrock	08/10	09/04	24/09	04/02	02/01	21/01	26/11	31/03		05/11	23/08	17/12	10/09	03/12	07/01	15/10	27/09	18/02	03/03	17/03	27/08	21/04
Harrow Borough	21/04	27/08	23/08	29/10	31/03	25/02	04/02	10/09	10/03		24/09	02/01	14/01	01/10	12/11	03/12	17/12	26/11	17/03	04/10	09/04	28/01
Hastings United	19/11	07/01	21/01	24/03	10/03	03/09	07/04	12/11	31/12	14/04		08/10	29/10	13/09	27/09	26/12	10/12	29/08	28/04	11/02	25/02	20/08
Hendon	10/03	03/12	19/11	31/12	12/11	24/03	20/08	11/02	13/09	29/08	28/01		04/10	14/04	29/10	03/09	25/02	07/04	01/10	21/04	14/01	26/12
Horsham	24/03	04/02	05/11	20/08	21/04	13/09	08/10	03/12	07/04	27/09	18/02	21/01		31/12	26/12	29/08	07/01	03/09	15/10	03/03	26/11	14/04
Kingstonian	25/02	17/03	31/03	11/03	27/08	12/11	21/01	08/10	28/04	08/01	17/12	24/09	22/08		11/12	26/09	26/11	04/02	09/04	02/01	10/09	29/10
Leatherhead	03/12	31/03	17/03	28/01	24/09	04/02	15/10	27/08	01/10	03/03	14/01	18/02	09/04	21/04		26/11	10/09	05/11	02/01	23/08	17/12	04/10
Lewes	29/10	10/09	27/08	12/11	28/01	10/03	10/12	24/09	25/02	28/04	09/04	31/03	02/01	14/01	11/02		17/03	05/10	24/08	17/12	01/10	19/11
Lowestoft Town	29/08	03/03	03/12	26/12	04/10	14/04	03/09	19/11	14/01	13/09	21/04	15/10	01/10	11/02	07/04	20/08		24/03	05/11	18/02	28/01	31/12
Margate	27/09	23/08	21/04	25/02	03/12	08/10	07/01	09/04	29/10	11/02	02/01	10/09	31/03	19/11	10/03	21/01	27/08		17/12	24/09	17/03	12/11
Metropolitan Police	03/09	21/01	08/10	07/04	11/02	28/09	14/04	29/10	12/11	20/08	03/12	07/01	25/02	26/12	29/08	31/12	10/03	14/09		19/11	21/04	24/03
Tooting & Mitcham U.	07/04	08/10	07/01	28/04	25/02	26/12	24/03	28/09	20/08	21/01	26/11	10/12	12/11	29/08	31/12	14/09	29/10	14/04	04/02		10/03	03/09
Wealdstone	14/04	18/02	03/03	03/09	19/11	31/12	28/04	21/01	24/03	26/12	15/10	26/09	11/02	07/04	12/09	07/01	08/10	20/08	10/12	05/11		29/08
Wingate & Finchley	07/01	15/10	27/09	26/11	10/09	28/04	05/11	17/12	10/12	11/10	17/03	09/04	24/09	18/02	21/01	04/02	23/08	03/03	27/08	31/03	02/01	

Ryman Football League Division One North 2011/2012 Fixtures

	AFC Sudbury	Brentwood Town	Chatham Town	Cheshunt	Enfield Town	Grays Athletic	Great Wakering Rovers	Harlow Town	Heybridge Swifts	Ilford	Leiston	Maldon & Tiptree	Needham Market	Potters Bar Town	Redbridge	Romford	Soham Town Rangers	Thamesmead Town	Tilbury	Waltham Abbey	Waltham Forest	Ware
AFC Sudbury		10/03	29/10	04/10	12/11	31/03	25/02	10/09	28/04	23/08	14/01	17/12	02/01	01/10	17/03	10/12	09/04	24/09	27/08	26/11	28/01	04/02
Brentwood Town	05/11		07/01	17/12	27/09	24/09	19/11	27/08	15/10	09/04	03/03	02/01	03/12	22/10	21/04	11/02	31/03	23/08	17/03	10/09	18/02	21/01
Chatham Town	18/02	01/10		27/08	19/11	10/09	11/02	23/08	22/10	31/03	05/11	17/03	21/04	28/01	03/12	04/10	17/12	09/04	02/01	24/09	14/01	03/03
Cheshunt	21/01	17/09	24/03		14/04	07/01	20/08	29/10	10/12	12/11	31/12	25/02	15/10	26/12	19/11	07/04	10/03	27/09	11/02	28/04	13/09	29/08
Enfield Town	03/03	14/01	04/02	24/09		03/12	28/01	31/03	18/02	17/03	21/04	27/08	10/09	04/10	02/01	01/10	26/11	17/12	23/08	09/04	22/10	05/11
Grays Athletic	14/09	14/04	07/04	01/10	28/04		29/08	25/02	24/03	10/03	17/09	28/01	11/02	19/11	14/01	26/12	12/11	29/10	05/10	10/12	31/12	20/08
Great Wakering Rov.	22/10	04/02	26/11	17/03	15/10	02/01		17/12	03/03	21/01	18/02	23/08	31/03	05/11	10/09	28/04	24/09	27/08	09/04	07/01	10/12	27/09
Harlow Town	07/04	24/03	31/12	18/02	13/09	22/10	17/09		19/11	03/12	28/01	04/10	05/11	29/08	11/02	20/08	01/10	21/04	14/01	03/03	14/04	26/12
Heybridge Swifts	03/12	28/01	25/02	21/04	29/10	27/08	12/11	04/02		17/12	04/10	09/04	23/08	14/01	24/09	10/03	10/09	17/03	31/03	02/01	01/10	26/11
Ilford	31/12	26/12	14/09	03/03	20/08	05/11	05/10	28/04	17/09		24/03	26/11	22/10	07/04	28/01	14/01	10/12	04/02	01/10	18/02	29/08	14/04
Leiston	27/09	12/11	10/03	23/08	10/12	17/12	29/10	15/10	21/01	27/08		24/09	09/04	28/04	31/03	25/02	02/01	26/11	10/09	17/03	04/02	07/01
Maldon & Tiptree	17/09	29/08	20/08	22/10	24/03	15/10	31/12	21/01	26/12	11/02	14/04		27/09	03/03	18/02	19/11	28/04	07/01	10/12	05/11	07/04	13/09
Needham Market	29/08	28/04	10/12	28/01	07/04	26/11	13/09	10/03	31/12	25/02	26/12	14/01		20/08	01/10	14/04	04/10	12/11	29/10	04/02	24/03	17/09
Potters Bar Town	07/01	25/02	15/10	09/04	21/01	04/02	10/03	02/01	27/09	10/09	03/12	12/11	17/03		17/12	29/10	23/08	31/03	24/09	27/08	26/11	21/04
Redbridge	20/08	10/12	28/04	04/02	29/08	27/09	07/04	26/11	14/04	15/10	13/09	29/10	07/01	17/09		31/12	25/02	10/03	12/11	21/01	26/12	24/03
Romford	21/04	26/11	21/01	10/09	07/01	09/04	03/12	17/03	05/11	27/09	22/10	04/02	24/09	18/02	23/08		27/08	02/01	17/12	31/03	03/03	15/10
Soham Town Rang.	26/12	13/09	17/09	05/11	11/02	03/03	14/04	07/01	07/04	21/04	29/08	03/12	21/01	31/12	22/10	24/03		15/10	19/11	27/09	20/08	18/02
Thamesmead Town	14/04	31/12	26/12	14/01	17/09	18/02	24/03	10/12	20/08	19/11	11/02	01/10	03/03	13/09	05/11	29/08	28/01		28/04	22/10	04/10	07/04
Tilbury	24/03	20/08	29/08	26/11	31/12	21/01	26/12	27/09	13/09	07/01	07/04	21/04	18/02	14/04	03/03	17/09	04/02	03/12		15/10	05/11	22/10
Waltham Abbey	11/02	07/04	14/04	03/12	26/12	21/04	01/10	12/11	29/08	29/10	20/08	10/03	19/11	24/03	04/10	13/09	14/01	25/02	28/01		17/09	31/12
Waltham Forest	15/10	29/10	28/09	31/03	25/02	24/08	21/04	24/09	07/01	02/01	19/11	10/09	27/08	11/02	09/04	12/11	17/03	21/01	10/03	17/12		03/12
Ware	19/11	04/10	12/11	02/01	10/03	17/03	14/01	09/04	11/02	24/09	01/10	31/03	17/12	10/12	27/08	28/01	29/10	10/09	25/02	23/08	28/04	

Ryman Football League Division One South 2011/2012 Fixtures

	Bognor Regis Town	Burgess Hill Town	Chipstead	Corinthian-Casuals	Crawley Down	Croydon Athletic	Dulwich Hamlet	Eastbourne Town	Faversham Town	Folkestone Invicta	Godalming Town	Hythe Town	Maidstone United	Merstham	Ramsgate	Sittingbourne	Walton & Hersham	Walton Casuals	Whitehawk	Whitstable Town	Whyteleafe	Worthing
Bognor Regis Town		05/11	20/08	21/01	13/09	31/12	27/09	19/11	15/10	03/03	01/11	24/03	03/12	11/02	07/01	07/04	21/04	18/02	29/08	17/09	14/04	26/12
Burgess Hill Town	10/03		13/09	24/03	26/12	20/08	28/04	12/11	04/02	07/01	26/11	14/04	27/09	25/02	29/10	17/09	31/12	15/10	21/01	10/12	07/04	29/08
Chipstead	17/03	31/03		29/10	14/01	01/10	10/09	25/02	17/12	21/04	09/04	28/01	24/09	23/08	27/08	10/03	04/10	02/01	03/12	12/11	11/02	19/11
Corinthian-Casuals	04/10	27/08	18/02		03/03	14/01	02/01	17/12	03/12	23/08	10/09	01/10	09/04	17/03	31/03	19/11	28/01	24/09	21/04	11/02	22/10	05/11
Crawley Down	31/03	09/04	27/09	12/11		26/11	23/08	02/01	21/01	10/09	24/09	29/10	27/08	17/12	17/03	25/02	10/03	07/01	04/02	15/10	21/04	03/12
Croydon Athletic	24/08	17/03	07/01	28/09	11/02		09/04	27/08	02/01	03/12	17/12	25/02	10/09	24/09	21/04	29/10	12/11	31/03	15/10	10/03	19/11	21/1
Dulwich Hamlet	14/01	03/12	07/04	29/08	31/12	26/12		01/10	21/04	05/11	28/01	17/09	18/02	04/10	19/11	11/02	22/10	14/04	13/09	20/08	03/03
Eastbourne Town	04/02	03/03	22/10	17/09	29/08	24/03	07/01		27/09	21/01	03/12	13/09	05/11	21/04	15/10	20/08	14/04	26/11	26/12	07/04	31/12	18/02
Faversham Town	28/01	19/11	17/09	28/04	04/10	29/08	10/12	14/01		18/02	03/03	31/12	22/10	01/10	11/02	26/12	07/04	05/11	24/03	14/04	13/09	20/08
Folkestone Invicta	12/11	01/10	10/12	31/12	07/04	28/04	10/03	05/10	29/10		14/01	26/12	26/11	28/01	25/02	14/04	20/08	04/02	17/09	29/08	24/03	14/09
Godalming Town	25/02	11/02	26/12	07/04	14/04	17/09	15/10	28/04	12/11	27/09		20/08	07/01	29/10	10/03	10/12	24/03	21/01	13/09	19/11	29/08	31/12
Hythe Town	27/08	24/09	15/10	07/01	18/02	08/10	17/12	31/03	23/08	09/04	17/03		21/01	03/12	02/01	11/02	19/11	10/09	03/03	27/09	05/11	21/04
Maidstone United	28/04	14/01	14/04	26/12	24/03	07/04	29/10	10/03	25/02	11/02	01/10	05/10		19/11	12/11	30/08	14/09	10/12	20/08	31/12	28/01	17/09
Merstham	26/11	22/10	31/12	20/08	17/09	14/04	21/01	10/12	07/01	15/10	18/02	28/04	04/02		27/09	13/09	29/08	03/03	05/11	24/03	26/12	07/04
Ramsgate	01/10	18/02	24/03	13/09	20/08	10/12	04/02	28/01	26/11	22/10	05/11	29/08	03/03	14/01		31/12	17/09	28/04	07/04	26/12	04/10	14/04
Sittingbourne	10/09	17/12	05/11	04/02	22/10	18/02	27/08	17/03	09/04	24/09	21/04	26/11	02/01	31/03	23/08		03/12	27/09	07/01	21/01	03/03	15/10
Walton & Hersham	10/12	23/08	21/01	15/10	05/11	03/03	26/11	24/09	10/09	17/03	27/08	04/02	31/03	02/01	17/12	28/04		09/04	22/10	07/01	18/02	27/09
Walton Casuals	29/10	28/01	29/08	14/04	01/10	13/09	25/02	10/03	19/11	04/10	07/04	21/04	12/11	03/12	14/01	26/12		31/12	20/08	17/09	24/03
Whitehawk	02/01	04/10	28/04	10/12	19/11	28/01	24/09	09/04	27/08	17/12	31/03	12/11	17/03	10/03	10/09	01/10	25/02	23/08		29/10	14/01	11/02
Whitstable Town	17/12	21/04	03/03	26/11	28/01	05/11	31/03	10/09	24/09	02/01	04/02	14/01	23/08	27/08	09/04	04/10	01/10	17/03	18/02		03/12	22/10
Whyteleafe	24/09	10/09	26/11	25/02	10/12	04/02	17/03	23/08	31/03	27/08	02/01	10/03	15/10	09/04	21/01	12/11	29/10	17/12	27/09	28/04		07/01
Worthing	09/04	02/01	04/02	10/03	28/04	04/10	12/11	29/10	17/03	31/03	23/08	10/12	17/12	10/09	24/09	28/01	14/01	27/08	26/11	25/02	01/10	

Also available from Soccer Books Ltd. –

THE FIRST 100 YEARS

OF THE ISTHMIAN FOOTBALL LEAGUE

NICK ROBINSON

This large-sized, well-produced book charts the first 100 years of the Isthmian Football League (which is currently sponsored by Rymans). This book is packed with statistics including the result of every game played in the League and final League tables together with a brief season-by-season review and a number of team photographs plus other images.

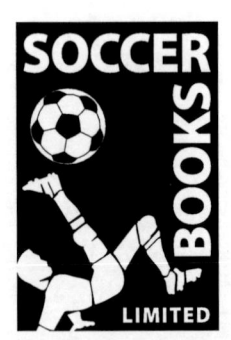

Softback Price £ 19.95

UK Postage £7.00 • Surface Postage £12.50 • Airmail £16.50

SOCCER BOOKS LIMITED
72 ST. PETERS AVENUE
CLEETHORPES,   DN35 8HU
UNITED KINGDOM

Web site–   www.soccer-books.co.uk

Football League Tables & Non-League Football Tables

AVAILABLE FROM WWW.SUPPORTERSGUIDES.COM

978-1-86223-218-1

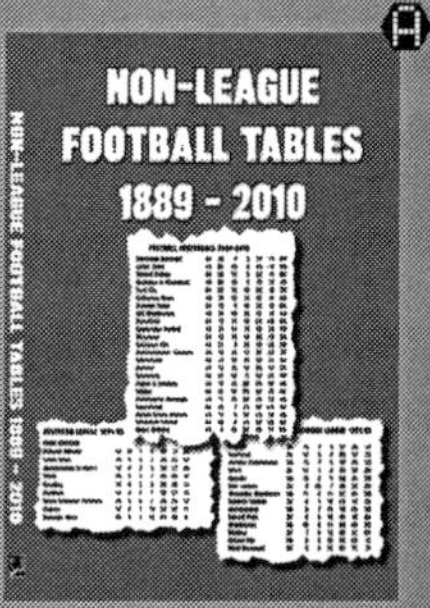

978-1-86223-204-4

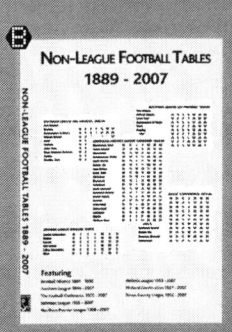

978-1-86223-162-7

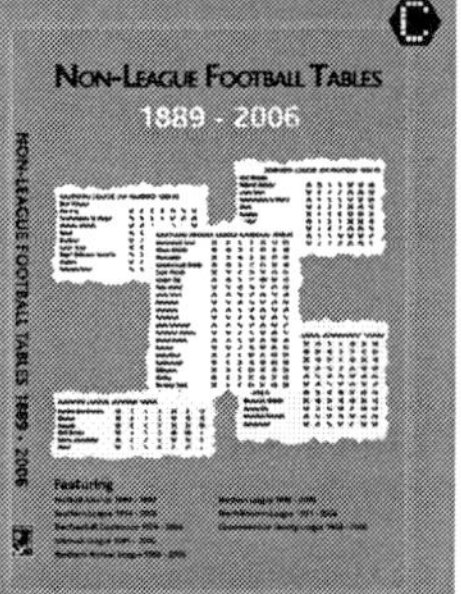

978-1-86223-144-3

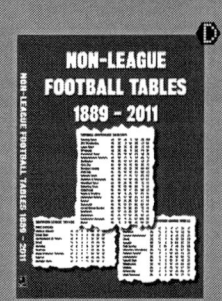

978-1-86223-217-4

ALL NON-LEAGUE FOOTBALL TABLES BOOKS FEATURE THE FOLLOWING LEAGUES:

- Isthmian League
- Football Alliance
- Southern League
- Football Conference
- Northern Premier League

ADDITIONAL LEAGUES FEATURED:

(B)
- Sussex County League
- The Essex Senior League
- The Northern Counties East League
- The Central League
- The Midland Combination

(E)
- Hellenic League
- Midland Combination
- Devon County League

(C)
- Western League
- South Western League
- Gloucestershire County League

(D)
- United Counties League
- The East Midlands League
- The Welsh Premier League
- The United League
- The Central Amateur League
- The Central Combination
- The Lancashire League
- The Combination

ISBN 978-1-86223-216-7

£9.95

Supporters' Guides Series

This top-selling series has been published since 1982 and the new editions contain the 2010/2011 Season's results and tables, Directions, Photographs, Telephone numbers, Parking information, Admission details, Disabled information and much more.

THE SUPPORTERS' GUIDE TO PREMIER & FOOTBALL LEAGUE CLUBS 2012

This 28th edition covers all 92 Premiership and Football League clubs.   *Price £7.99*

NON-LEAGUE SUPPORTERS' GUIDE AND YEARBOOK 2012

This 20th edition covers all 68 clubs in Step 1 & Step 2 of Non-League football – the Football Conference National, Conference North and Conference South.   *Price £7.99*

SCOTTISH FOOTBALL SUPPORTERS' GUIDE AND YEARBOOK 2012

The 19th edition featuring all Scottish Premier League, Scottish League and Highland League clubs.   *Price £6.99*

RYMAN FOOTBALL LEAGUE SUPPORTERS' GUIDE AND YEARBOOK 2012

This 2nd edition features the 66 clubs which make up the 3 divisions of the Isthmian League, sponsored by Ryman.   *Price £6.99*

THE EVO-STIK LEAGUE SOUTHERN SUPPORTERS' GUIDE AND YEARBOOK 2012

This 2nd edition features the 66 clubs which make up the 3 divisions of the Southern Football League, sponsored by Evo-Stik.   *Price £6.99*

THE EVO-STIK NORTHERN PREMIER LEAGUE SUPPORTERS' GUIDE AND YEARBOOK 2012

This 2nd edition features the 67 clubs which make up the 3 divisions of the Northern Premier League, sponsored by Evo-Stik.   *Price £6.99*

THE SUPPORTERS' GUIDE TO WELSH FOOTBALL 2011

The enlarged 12th edition covers the 112+ clubs which make up the top 3 tiers of Welsh Football.   *Price £8.99*

These books are available UK & Surface post free from –

Soccer Books Limited (Dept. SBL)
72 St. Peter's Avenue
Cleethorpes,   DN35 8HU
United Kingdom